The
Seduction of
POWER

The Seduction of POWER

Ed Dobson and Ed Hindson

Fleming H. Revell Company
Old Tappan, New Jersey

Unless otherwise identified, Scripture quotations in this book are taken from the King James Version of the Bible.

Scripture texts identified NIV are from the Holy Bible: New International Version, copyright © 1973, 1978, 1984 International Bible Society. Used by permission of Zondervan Bible Publishers.

Library of Congress Cataloging-in-Publication Data

Dobson, Ed.
   The seduction of power : preachers, politics, and the media / Ed Dobson and Ed Hindson.
        p.   cm.
   Bibliography: p.
   ISBN 0-8007-1606-X
        1. Evangelicalism—United States—History—20th century. 2. Conservatism—United States—History—20th century.   3. Christianity and politics. 4. Power (Christian theology). 5. Television in religion—United States. 6. Evangelists—United States—History—20th century. 7. United States—Church history—20th century. 8. United States—Politics and government—1981–.   9. United States—Politics and government— 1945–. I. Hindson, Edward E. II. Title.
   BR1642.U5D63 1988
   277.3′0828—dc19   88-15555
                                                                                  CIP

Copyright © 1988 by Edward Dobson and Edward E. Hindson
Published by the Fleming H. Revell Company
Old Tappan, New Jersey 07675
Printed in the United States of America

TO
RICHARD JOHN NEUHAUS
Pastor, theologian, friend,
and defender of democracy

Contents

Reprinted by permission of John Trever, *Albuquerque Journal*.

Foreword

The British statesman Benjamin Disraeli observed in 1826 that "all power is a trust; that we are accountable for its exercise; that from the people, and for the people all springs, and all must exist."

In the pursuit, attainment, and exercise of power, Disraeli's definition ought to be uppermost in our minds. Failure to acknowledge the source of power and failure to handle it properly is what produces despots and despotic behavior.

To say that all power is a trust implies a source from which power flows. In Psalms 21:13, David acknowledges the power source: "Be thou exalted, Lord, in thine own strength: so will we sing and praise thy power."

Acknowledging God as the source and giver of power is a prerequisite to handling power. Without such acknowledgment we are leaving ourselves open to being corrupted by power.

As with a borrowed library book, we are accountable for how we handle something that belongs to someone else. The lack of accountability among those in the so-called "Religious Right" has been the fundamental flaw in the entire movement and has led, I believe, to its rapid dissipation as a national political force.

When power is seized, rather than conferred by the people, it resembles a coup d'état rather than an inauguration. This is why it is so important to build a consensus so that power might have legitimacy. Unfortunately, the "Religious Right" appeared to be more interested in the exercise of power and the attention it brought

9

to the movement and its leaders than it was in building a cultural and political consensus around a defensible agenda of compelling issues. The issues were right and proper. The way they were argued was often superficial and seemed self-serving.

That power can be dangerous is no excuse for returning to the political catacombs. Without a vision the people perish and who better to posit a vision than those who know that the principles in the Scripture work for individuals and nations?

But the Christian community should have learned a valuable lesson as it viewed in all its ignominy what happens when men and women abuse power. Now it is important to take that lesson and to ask what must be done to properly and biblically exercise power to achieve, as the Founders wrote in the Constitution's Preamble, "a more perfect union," that will "promote the general welfare, provide for the common defense and insure domestic tranquility."

Notice that it is not a perfect Union that is to be promoted, but a "more perfect Union." Another way of putting it might be a "less sinful" or "more righteous" Union in which biblical values will be reflected from the inside out. I think that the reason the New Right was not more successful is that they were seen to be more intent in pursuing power as an end rather than as a means to the end of persuading people of the correctness of their position.

Inside American passports the State Department offers us the option of dual citizenship. We are warned that if we elect to declare ourselves dual citizens (citizens of America and of another country) we not only will enjoy whatever benefits we perceive there to be in such an arrangement, but we also may be required to exercise dual responsibilities. That is, we may be required to pay taxes to both countries and we may be required to serve in the armed forces of both nations.

It is apparent that insofar as many politically active Christians are concerned, our responsibility to God was eclipsed by the bright glare of publicity that came with our preoccupation with government.

Some felt that the political process could be used to shortcut God's process and usher in a spiritual revival on the wings of the Republican Party and on the broad shoulders of Ronald Reagan. The revelations by former White House Chief of Staff Donald Regan that the Reagans are guided more by astrology than by the Scriptures was the final letdown for the president's evangelical and fundamentalist followers.

The worst mistake that could be made is to give up on politics. Liberal Democrats did not drop out because Gary Hart disappointed them. We don't stop eating when we are served a bad meal or receive poor service.

So, where to go from here?

Ed Dobson and Ed Hindson show the way. They should know. They were present at the creation of the New Right and saw its good side and downside.

As I have read the history of revivals in America, I have been impressed that God acted not when His people were in positions of power and authority or when the "right man" was in the White House and the Congress and Supreme Court were controlled by the "right" party and philosophy. God acted when men and women were at their weakest and when all appeared to be lost without His intervention. When men began to pray and to cry out to God to rescue them from lawlessness and anarchy is when God moved. He is like that. Not willing to share His glory with anyone, God waits until man is so desperate that he can take no credit at all for what God is about to do.

Have we reached that point as a nation at the end of the twentieth century? I don't know. Our pride is very strong. Though we place "In God We Trust" on our money, if it were true that we really did trust in God, another revival (the last was in 1905) would have swept our country before now.

As I search the Scriptures, I read that God's strength is made perfect in weakness; that if I humble myself under the mighty hand of God, He will exalt me if I do not faint; that those who wish to lead must first learn to serve; that those who wait upon the Lord will renew their strength and that the power of God's Spirit is far greater than the power of the ways of men.

In thinking of these things and of what is to follow in this book, we would do well to put our priorities in order and to remember what Eric Liddel said in the movie *Chariots of Fire:* "Where does the power come from to run the race? It comes from within.'' We would do even better to remember what Jesus Christ said in what has come to be called ''The Lord's Prayer,'' but what is really a prayer for the Disciples who had asked Him how they should pray: ''. . . for thine is the kingdom and the power and the glory forever.''

—Cal Thomas
Washington, D.C.
May 1988

PREFACE

The quest for power is certainly nothing new to human history. Ancient man faced it at the dawn of creation when Satan implied that he could make him like God. The Romans were intoxicated with power and defined their chief deity, Zeus, as the god of power. At Pergamum in Asia Minor, they built a great altar and temple to this god of power and deified their emperors as an act of the worship of power. It is no wonder that the Apostle John called the place "Satan's seat" (Revelation 2:13).

Power, especially political power, is something that has always eluded evangelical Christians. We tend to view ourselves as a spiritual minority—pilgrims journeying through the vast secular wasteland of life. Historically, we have made little attempt to gain or even influence political power. Rather, we have generally been content to evangelize the lost, disciple the faithful, and neglect the rest.

But all of that changed drastically in 1980, and things have not been the same since. Many of us came charging into the public arena of politics and found that we did have some power and influence after all. In fact, we liked our newfound power and, all too quickly, some of us became intoxicated by it. Preachers who began talking about principles got caught up talking about party politics. People concerned about spiritual convictions became more interested in particular candidates.

A subtle shift began to take place. The seduction of power was luring us into the quicksands of pride, arrogance, and self-

13

sufficiency. Then the bottom dropped out. Now many evangelicals find themselves embarrassed and confused, wondering about the way ahead. Some want to press on, while others insist that we have gone too far already. Most are asking, Where do we go from here?

This book is a modest attempt to answer that question. We hope that we have learned from our experiences so that we have a better grasp on the whole issue of religion, politics, and the media. Both of us were involved in the early phases of the development of the New Right. We were caught up in the euphoria of its early success. But, in time, we began to question its real effectiveness and its ultimate direction.

Unlike those who want to give up on any Christian influence in politics, we believe there is still a great potential in this enterprise if we can clarify our goals, methods, and motives. We cannot hope to transform society by isolating ourselves from it. But if we are to make a difference in this world, it will only be by the power of God.

Ed Dobson   Ed Hindson
Calvary Church   National Religious Broadcasters
Grand Rapids, Michigan   Morristown, New Jersey
                     Easter 1988

14

The
Seduction of
POWER

Chapter One

The Gospel
According to Power

*Not by might, nor by power, but by my spirit, saith
the Lord of hosts.*

Zechariah 4:6

Evangelical religion has fallen on hard times
these days. Its problems have not resulted
from the pursuit of the religious but of the
political and material. Ironically, the one force
which should have been the most resistant to
the seduction of power has fallen victim to it. Our initial success in
confronting the social and political power structures of our society
may well have caused us to lower our guard against temptation
ourselves.

We who so desperately want to see society come to repentance
need to repent ourselves. The high visibility which the media have
given the New Right may well have undermined our spiritual
integrity in the process, because it has tempted us to sin in our
own areas of spiritual weakness: pride, dissension, and the lust
for power.

It was Harvey Cox who first accused modern religion of spiritual seduction.[1] He observed that *to seduce* means to "mislead or
deceive." He warned that "the great seducers of history all had
one thing in common: they could use the natural needs and instincts of another person for their own selfish ends." He argued
that seduction is the most callous form of exploitation because "it

17

tricks the victim into becoming an unwitting accomplice in his own seduction.''

The real tragedy for evangelicals is that many of us seduced ourselves into thinking that we could really make a difference in society, but we squandered our window of opportunity. The public moral failures of Jim Bakker and Jimmy Swaggart have left the general public cynically questioning if anyone is for real. In the meantime, the resultant ecclesiastical bickering has caused many to turn away from the Church altogether, although at least one news commentator has remarked, ''All of this is almost enough to make me believe in God again.''

Cal Thomas has argued that the New Right is in danger of capitulating to the same temptation that ensnared left wing liberal religion when it began to view government as its first resource and God as its last resort.[2] The end result is that religion becomes pathetic, rather than prophetic. It fails to speak the truth to power, while attempting to elicit favor to further its own agenda. As a result, the political parties tend to treat evangelicals as just another special interest group, rather than people who really speak for God. We diminish the truth claims of Christianity and leave the Bride of Christ lusting after other suitors.

The current evangelical scene is one of confusion over the issue of religion and politics. Jerry Falwell announced that he was getting out of politics, while Pat Robertson announced that he was running for president. Reconstructionists are calling for the establishment of a Christian theocracy. Pietists, on the other hand, want to avoid any connection with politics whatever. Separatists refuse to cooperate in political issues with those who differ from them theologically. Left wing evangelicals differ politically from right wing evangelicals. It would seem for the moment that everyone is confused. Add to this mix the moral breakdown of Bakker and Swaggart and the disillusionment with televangelism in general, and one can't help but wonder where it is all headed.

Evangelical Christianity is a vibrant spiritual movement that is a significant part of the religious tapestry of America. It has grown to an enormous size while going virtually unobserved by the public at large. Its emphasis traditionally has been on evangelism and spiritual growth. Evangelicals are newcomers to politics and public policy debate. They entered the public arena as a backlash against the growing power of secularism in American public life.

THE POWERFUL AND THE POWERLESS

Religion has always had a precarious relationship to political power. When power is on the side of religion, it tends to corrupt it. But when power is against religion, it tends to persecute it. Unfortunately, the pressure of persecution often drives religion to desire power as a means of protection and self-preservation. But in time, religion has often used power to persecute as well. Thus it has fallen victim to the very thing it opposed. It was C. S. Lewis who said that once we give up our souls to gain power, we become enslaved to that to which we have given ourselves.

This problem is certainly not a new one. The Jews of Jesus' day struggled with the seductive temptations of power as well. In fact, they were neatly divided in their attitudes toward power.

The **Herodians** were the Jewish party that favored the rule of Herod and his cooperation with the Romans as the best possible means of dealing with the political power of Rome. The Roman emperor Augustus allowed Herod to retain the title of king as long as he used his powers to further Augustus's control of Judea. Jesus' warning about the "leaven of Herod" (Mark 8:15) undoubtedly applies to the Herodians' desire for a political Messiah, even if he were a secular one.[3]

The **Sadducees** were a priestly class who considered themselves the true priests of Israel. They had little popular support but formed an elitist group of Judean Hellenists. They had been favored by the Hasmonean rulers and dominated the Sanhedrin in Jesus' time. They were the political realists of their day and were consumed with keeping Roman political power at bay by cooperation and even compromise when necessary.[4]

The **Pharisees** were the religious legalists and separatists of the New Testament era. They were the spiritual descendants of Ezra and sought to control the religion of the Jewish state by demanding the strict observance of Mosaic Law. As early as the second century

B.C., they were known as *hasidim* ("separated ones"). They fell into bad times under the later Hasmonean rulers, however, and Herod became increasingly hostile toward them because of their resistance to his promotion of Hellenistic culture. After Herod's death, they appealed to direct Roman rule and opposed the revolt against Rome. Interestingly, Jesus also warned against the "leaven of the Pharisees" (Mark 8:15) because they sought a Messiah who would overthrow the Romans and set up a theocracy in Israel.[5]

The **Essenes** were a priestly and monastic community of religious pietists who rejected traditional Temple religion and viewed themselves as an exiled community of true believers. The term *essenoi* means "holy ones." Josephus states that they were totally apolitical and were content to wait for the coming of the Messiah. Therefore, their writings were very apocalyptic in nature. They saw a spiritual Messiah eradicating the powers of darkness as the only true hope for the world. Thus they had no interest in influencing the politics or public policy formation of Roman Judea.[6]

The **Zealots** were the opposite of the Essenes. They were patriotic Israelite fanatics who believed God wanted them to be His instruments to overthrow the Roman government. The New Testament indicates that there was considerable popular sentiment for their beliefs. As a political party, they were founded by Judas the Galilean, who led a revolt against Rome in A.D. 6. They opposed payment of tribute by Israel to a pagan emperor as treason against God. It was their desire to follow the example of the Maccabeans, who manifested zeal for the Law of God when they revolted against the Greeks in the second century B.C. Zealotry grew among the people after Emperor Claudius had the Jews banned from Rome in A.D. 50 and finally culminated in the Jewish Revolt against Rome in A.D. 66–70. The last Zealot stronghold, Masada, fell in A.D. 73. There can be no doubt that it was the popular spirit of zealotry, not spirituality, that provoked the people to want to make Jesus their king.[7]

Jesus' preaching of the Kingdom of God contradicted every prevailing view of religion and politics in His day. He rejected the asceticism and isolationism of the Essenes. He refused to play the games of political accommodation that characterized the Sadducees and Pharisees. He totally confounded the Herodians and refused to give cause to the Zealots. He stood alone with a uniquely new message, emphasizing that the Kingdom of God was within the hearts of true believers. Thus, they were free from the suppression of political domination or the corruption of political compromise. They were citizens of heaven as well as earth, and their mission on earth was to make people citizens of the Kingdom of God.

Jesus offered the people of His day a whole new way of looking at politics and power. He clearly announced, "My kingdom is not of this world" (John 18:36). But ironically, His own disciples have always struggled with this issue. At the time of His ascension, they asked, "Wilt thou at this time restore again the kingdom to Israel?" (Acts 1:6). He reminded them that He had another priority and that was the preaching of the Gospel to the whole world (Acts 1:8). By the end of the Book of Acts we find the Apostle Paul "preaching the kingdom of God" (Acts 28:31) free from all political entanglement.[8]

In time, the very government of Rome that had persecuted Jews and Christians alike became Christian under Constantine in the fourth century A.D. One would expect that those who had been so severely persecuted that they were driven into the catacombs would have resisted the temptation to misuse power themselves, but they did not. It was not long until the powerless became the powerful, and the persecuted became the persecutor.[9]

The whole history of the Church reveals that the seduction of power has all too often drawn her off course from her spiritual mission. Wars have been fought, crusades undertaken, inquisitions established, and people burned at the stake because someone capitulated to the illusion that spiritual goals could be accomplished by political means. When the Church has seized power in the name of Christ, the very principles of Christ have often been destroyed.

THE ILLUSION OF POWER

Power is one of the basic realities of life. People desire it as an opportunity to force their will on others or to keep others from forcing their will on them. It is the latter factor that has often provoked Christians to seek power, if for no other reason than to get others to leave them alone. Perhaps it is the dismal memory of the catacombs or the frightful experiences of persecution that cause us to fear power when it is held by anti-Christian forces. Though few of us have ever experienced such things ourselves, we know they are all too real for believers in other places.

Jacques Ellul has argued very forcibly that the subversion of Christianity occurs whenever we confuse spiritual authority with political power.[10] Especially in the case of state religion, when the Church embraces all of society, it baptizes the political and the social without necessarily transforming it. Thus it should not surprise us that the pursuit of power can become a morally corrupting process.

It has often been said that power corrupts and that absolute power corrupts absolutely. In his classic, *The Prince,* Machiavelli said that power and deception go hand in hand.

> A prince will never lack for legitimate excuses to explain away his breaches of faith. Modern history will furnish innumerable examples of this behavior, showing how the man succeeded best who knew best how to play the fox. But it is a necessary part of this nature that you must conceal it carefully; you must be a great liar and hypocrite. Men are so simple of mind, and so much dominated by their immediate needs, that a deceitful man will always find plenty who are ready to be deceived.[11]

Charles Colson has stated, "The history of the last fifty years has validated Nietzsche's argument that man's desire to control his own destiny and to impose his will on others is the most basic human motivation."[12] Nietzsche argued that the "will of power" would eventually fill the vacuum of values in the modern world, and he was right! We are now witnessing the culmination of the deterioration of Western culture. For nearly a century, modern man has been told that he is an animal, and now he is starting to live like one. But like an animal, he has no allegiance to the morals or values of the past. Modern man has struck out on his own, and he is adrift on the sea of relativity.

The great danger of our times is that someone will attempt to grab the power from the vacuum of American life and use it to his or her own ends. Ironically, religious people fear that is exactly what secularists are attempting to do, while secularists are accusing religionists of the same thing.

In his landmark study, *Power,* Adolf Berle stated, "Power and love are the oldest known phenomena of human emotions. Neither wholly yields to rational discussion."[13] He also observed, "Power is a universal experience; practically every adult has had a measure of it, great or small, for a brief moment or for an extended time."[14] But he also warned, "Except in rarest fortune, power leaves men before their lives are over."

Berle, professor emeritus of law at Columbia University, postulated five natural laws of power:[15]

1. Power fills any vacuum in human organization.
2. Power is invariably personal.
3. Power is based on a system of ideas or philosophy.
4. Power is exercised through, and depends on, institutions which limit and control it.
5. Power acts in relation to a field of responsibility.

Berle saw power as the human effort to confront chaos. He suggested that in any contest between power and chaos, power would always win. But he also acknowledged that such victories were always temporary in nature until the contest between power and chaos was renewed.

From a personal standpoint, Charles Colson has warned of the dangers of political power.[16] He has said that the hunger for political power lures people from the comfort of the private sector and drives them relentlessly in search of that which eventually eludes them. Colson's own experiences with the Nixon administration of the White House are ample testimony to the irrationality of this quest.

John Kotter has defined power as the measure of a person's potential to get others to do what he or she wants them to do, as well as being able to avoid doing what he or she does not want to do.[17] He warns that those at the top have little inherent security, since many factors that affect their performance are beyond their control.

Therefore he warns that the top executive is "constantly subject to the threat of disaster."[18] Personal integrity, he argues, is the key issue in the maintenance or loss of power. Unfortunately, it is the issue that the press has used to condemn evangelicals in general because of the failures of a few.

THE LURE OF PRIDE

Richard Foster states, "There is an intimate connection between pride and the destructive character of power."[19] He notes that the unholy trinity of pride, arrogance, and power destroyed Samson. His natural abilities and God-given gifts were taken for granted, and he soon found himself sacrificing his own principles for self-satisfying pleasure. Foster adds, "Among the dangerous people in our media-soaked culture are leaders who believe their own press releases." He notes that all of us are given to this temptation, but leaders are "especially susceptible today because of our infatuation with the media."[20]

The vanity of seeing oneself on television is incomparable with anything the world has ever known. Somehow we think that television defines our importance and that, in turn, determines our power. That is why it is so difficult for television preachers to maintain humility.

One sociologist recently commented on his impression of the sincerity of a certain televangelist and then added, "But I've seen him change over the years. He really seems to have been seduced by the power and the fame."[21]

The shocking events that led to the resignation of Jim Bakker from the PTL ministry and those that resulted in the disciplinary action brought against Jimmy Swaggart by the Assemblies of God ought to remind us that there are no superstars in God's work. God will not share His glory with another. Dr. Ben Armstrong, executive director of the National Religious Broadcasters, said recently, "Whenever ministers of the gospel, whether they are on television or not, start thinking they can bend the rules, they are sadly mistaken."[22] The Apostle Paul reminds us, "If a man also strive for masteries, yet is he not crowned, except he strive lawfully" (2 Timothy 2:5). In other words, keeping the rules is part of playing the game.

The current crisis must become a learning experience for all of us. The general public is now demanding greater accountability for their donations to radio and television ministries. This is a time for serious soul-searching, reevaluation, and positive action. We must set our house in order by initiating changes that will insure integrity and accountability if we are to regain our effectiveness.

Television is both a wonderful and difficult medium to master. The very nature of it can engender vanity and self-promotion. It is expensive and can push the religious broadcaster beyond the limits of reason in the attempt to raise funds. It is also powerful, and its power can easily corrupt the best of men. But used properly under the guidance of the Holy Spirit, for the glory of God, and the promotion of the Church of Jesus Christ, it can be the most wonderful and effective tool of evangelism ever known to mankind.

THE INFLUENCE OF TELEVISION

Television is *the* national pastime in America. We spend more time watching it than any other activity except sleeping. It has changed our ideas about marriage, family life, personal morality, and even politics. Television, more than any other aspect of our culture, sets the agenda for our society. It tells us what is important and meaningful in our lives. In many cases, it even determines when we get up and when we go to bed.

In their national best-seller, *Remote Control: Television and the Manipulation of American Life,* Frank Mankiewicz and Joel Swerdlow stated, "Television is more powerful than any other institution in America today."[23] They observed: "A best-selling book may reach several million people . . . a hit movie is seen by perhaps 6 million people. . . . The nation's largest-circulation newspaper has 2 million readers. But a television program which enters less than 30 million homes is a failure."[24]

Ninety-seven percent of all American households have at least one television set, more than are equipped with refrigerators or indoor toilets. The average American watches nearly four hours of television per day, meaning that he or she will spend nine years of life in front of a television set. By the time a youngster reaches the age of fifteen, he or she will witness twelve thousand acts of violence on television. The authors of *Remote Control* observe that, "If one wishes to see fifty-four acts of violence, one can watch all the plays of Shakespeare, or one can watch three evenings (sometimes only two) of prime-time television."[25]

Most of us who were raised on television from our earliest childhood do not think in the same patterns as did our parents or grandparents before us. According to one study, "The Television Generation consists roughly of all people born since 1945."[26] By 1990, nearly 75 percent of the total population will be members of the Television Generation. It is this generation that urged that one school give Captain Kangaroo an honorary doctorate and that the actor who played television doctor Marcus Welby be invited to speak at a medical school commencement!

Alistair Cooke observed, "Television has produced a generation of children who have a declining grasp of the English language, but have a visual sophistication that was denied to their parents."[27] Unfortunately, he warns, the power of televised images appeals more to the emotions than the intellect and bypasses critical aspects of judgment.

In 1938, author E. B. White predicted that television would become the test of the modern world. "We shall stand or fall by television," he warned.[28] While observing that television would expand our visual perception of reality, he also cautioned that the televised images would appear so real that, in time, we would no longer see the difference between the real and the unreal. Even the pain in another's face would leave "the impression of mere artifice."[29]

The power of televised images is so incredible, and yet so subtle, that most of us do not yet comprehend what they mean to our society. Harvey Cox observed in 1973 that the "new media, especially those dealing in pictorial images, are immensely powerful . . . TV reaches us at a level of consciousness below the critically centered intelligence."[30] He went on to observe that broadcast technology tends to make us all "quiescent consumers" victimized by the power of transmission. "Programs create, and then suggest ways to satisfy, human needs," he stated. "But the process is one of seduction."[31]

One of the great dangers of television is that it sends a message to the viewer that tells him he is getting what he wants and needs. Instead of meeting the viewer's real needs, mass media actually determine what those needs will be. Thus, it is no wonder that biblical prophecy speaks of the antichrist in terms of the "image of the beast" (Revelation 13:15).

THE NEED FOR REVIVAL

The New Right has lived by the media, and now is in danger of being crucified by it. National columnist William Safire has criticized fundamentalists as a faltering political force "biting down on its own moral toothache."[32] He accuses the New Right of pragmatically jumping from issue to issue without any serious commitment to change society.

Os Guinness has observed that the Church and society are "the test bed that reveals the character and health of all our truths. If we don't demonstrate them out in the crucible of society, we can take it they mean nothing, whatever we profess."[33] He asks if the glory has departed from the twentieth-century Church because of our lack of engagement in society in ways that are spiritually realistic and socially relevant.

Pastor and broadcaster Richard Lee of Atlanta has said, "In many ways the problems of Jim Bakker and Jimmy Swaggart are reflective of deeper problems within our entire society."[34] Our success in every area of life breeds what Charles Swindoll has called the quest for fortune, fame, power, and pleasure, rather than the quest for character.[35] America itself needs a spiritual revival of character and integrity on every level. Our national moral crisis touches nearly every aspect of our lives. Doctors, lawyers, politicians, and even preachers are affected.

Some have suggested that many of our problems result from sloppy and superficial sentimentality that often passes for evangelical theology.[36] Others have observed a dichotomy between belief

27

and practice.[37] Yet looming over all these issues is the seductive lure of power itself. Evangelicals have often viewed themselves as a powerless minority in a secular society. But eventually a man ran for president claiming to be "born again." Jimmy Carter's announcement in 1976 jolted the media into paying attention. Soon 1976 was declared the "Year of the Evangelical." The Gallup Poll declared that there were at least thirty million born again evangelicals in America, and the sleeping giant awoke to its own press clippings.

In the meantime, fundamentalist pastor Jerry Falwell criticized Carter on his nationally televised broadcast of the *Old-Time Gospel Hour* for giving an interview to *Playboy* magazine. "The next day Jody Powell, Carter's press secretary, called me up and cussed me out!" Falwell claimed. "That's when I realized the potential political power of Christian broadcasting."[38]

Soon Falwell launched the Moral Majority, and others followed suit.[39] In a matter of months a loose coalition formed and was labeled the New Right by the press. Liberals screamed that it was a violation of the separation of Church and State, but nobody paid attention because the National Council of Churches had been doing the same thing for as long as anyone could remember. Several conservative candidates were swept into office, including Ronald Reagan, and a new era was born.

The Reagan years have now come to an end, and even his critics have to admit he has done a masterful job. Inflation and unemployment are down. The economy has boomed, and people have enjoyed general prosperity during these years. Yet most people are concerned about the future. They aren't sure we really have solved anything.

Like everyone else in our society, the Church is caught in this moment of apprehension as well. People are questioning whether our involvement has really been worth it, and even our leaders are asking, Where do we go from here? If we separate the spiritual from the social and political aspects of life, we lose all relevance to society. But if we emphasize the social to the exclusion of the spiritual, we lose the only absolute left in an already relativistic society.[40]

In the Great Commission, our Lord said, "All power [Greek,

exousia, ''authority''] is given unto me in heaven and in earth. Go ye therefore, and teach all nations . . . and, lo, I am with you alway, even unto the end of the world'' (Matthew 28:18–20). Notice that the power of authority was given to Him, not us. We are to take His Gospel to the world based on His merits, not our own. Then, in Acts 1:8, Jesus told His disciples, ''But ye shall receive power [Greek, *dunamis,* ''force''], after that the Holy Ghost is come upon you: and ye shall be witnesses unto me . . . unto the uttermost part of the earth.''

Notice the proper place of power in the Gospel. First, Jesus Christ alone has the authority to send us into the world, and He promises to be with us until the end of this age. Second, He empowers our witness by the baptism of the Holy Spirit, so that we will recognize that whatever power we seem to have in doing His work is not of ourselves, but of Him. This is the only transmission of power that can change the course of history, and it is not limited to political institutions, though it can transform every area of society.

Chapter Two

The Current Tension Between Religion and Politics

. . . Render therefore unto Caesar the things which are Caesar's; and unto God the things that are God's.
Matthew 22:21

 Just when the press was ready to pronounce the death of the Religious Right, Pat Robertson's bid for the White House had them scurrying to find his "invisible army." Robertson's initial success in the primaries had the attention of the secular press once again focused on the issue of religion and politics. Sociologist Jeffrey Hadden of the University of Virginia claims that the Religious Right has been thriving and could well become the dominant political power in America by the end of this century.[1]

Hadden argues that the movement is larger than any one person and that Falwell's resignation from politics has had little effect on what is "rapidly becoming the most vigorous socio-political movement in America."[2] The numbers of evangelicals are growing continually, while the more politically and theologically liberal mainline churches are in serious decline.[3] Virtually all objective assessments now project the growing power and influence of evangelical Christianity in American public life.

One evangelical pastor, James Montgomery Boice, has remarked,

"A new wind is blowing across the political landscape, the wind of a revived evangelical electorate seeking to uphold high moral values and justice."[4] Yet Boice expresses great concern over the fact that a politically involved Church is likely to take its agenda, methods, and authority from the world, and cease to hold the proclamation of the Gospel of Christ and the righteousness of God as its primary objectives.

Both the potential and peril of the power evangelicals exert on American public life are awesome. "Not since the so-called Scopes Monkey Trial in 1925 have American Evangelicals and Fundamentalists received so much public attention as they are getting in the mid-1980s," remarks Richard John Neuhaus. "Their churches are growing, their colleges and universities are expanding and their political influence is growing."[5]

THE PRESENT DANGER

After nearly a decade of public involvement in the political process, evangelicals are finally being understood as a social force that has been developing throughout the twentieth century. Their retirement from public life after the repeal of Prohibition paved the way for the heyday of liberal Protestant influence in American public policy during the era from 1930 to 1960. However, the evangelicals did not disappear from society altogether. Nor were they limited to cultural isolation in Appalachia. Instead, they were concentrating on evangelism and church growth during a time when the more liberal churches were focusing their efforts on social issues.[6]

The great danger, however, that exists for the Religious Right at this moment in history is to become intoxicated with its own power. "We have the numbers to make the difference," Pat Robertson has said.[7] "There is enough momentum that the evangelicals are not going to walk away from politics," Hadden observes.[8] But it is in just this context that power becomes so seductively attractive. We now have the votes to make the difference because we have concentrated on the basics of a spiritual ministry for over fifty years. We are not powerful because we have sought power, but because we have sought the Lord.

It is in this same manner that our Lord reminded Pilate, "My kingdom is not of this world" (John 18:36). When Pilate became frustrated in questioning Jesus, he threatened, "Knowest thou not that I have power to crucify thee, and have power to release thee?" To which our Lord replied, "Thou couldest have no power at all against me, except it were given thee from above" (John 19:10, 11).

The term "power" in this passage translates the Greek word *exousia* (power in the sense of authority). The more familiar word *dunamis* ("power" in the sense of force or might) is not used in this passage. Therefore, Christ is not threatening Pilate with a display of force, but, rather, He is reminding him that all human authority is delegated authority, whereas the *exousia* of God is absolute and unrestricted.[9] Thus true power in the world derives from divine authority and not from political force.

This is the vital truth to which evangelical Christians must adhere above all else. Might does not necessarily mean we are right. We have often viewed ourselves as a religious minority holding forth against the dragon of unrestricted secularism. Now the tables are turning in our favor. We may well have a greater voice of influence than ever before in this century. But we dare not blow the opportunity by becoming entangled in the mundane affairs of power politics and forgetting that true power (authority) is from God.[10] He is the ultimate source of authority and He communicates that authority to us when we determine to please Him. It is our spiritual success, based upon an adherence to His Word, that has resulted in our numerical growth and our political influence. As a result of that influence in the political arena, we are often compelled to justify one party or system over another. This has been especially difficult for evangelical missionaries caught between competing political systems in emerging nations of the Third World.

On the other hand, there is much to be said in favor of political involvement by the Christian community. Politics, simply defined, is the life of the city (*polis*) and the responsibilities of the citizen (*polites*). British evangelical John Stott states that in its broadest sense, politics is concerned with "the whole of our life in human society." Therefore, it is "the art of living together in community."

In a more narrow sense, he also observes, it is the "science of government" whereby the adoption of specific policies are "enshrined in legislation."[11] In this regard, he argues, true Christianity cannot, indeed it dare not, become isolated from society.

Richard Neuhaus has stated that "religion is the heart of culture, culture is the form of religion, and politics is a function of culture."[12] In this sense, religion and politics are inseparable expressions of human culture. He further argues that the culture-forming enterprise in America can be traced back to the nation's Puritan beginnings. However, he contends that evangelical Christians have been largely absent from the process of defining America or setting her moral agenda. But with the abdication of mainline religion from the task of legitimizing the American experiment, Neuhaus believes that the opportunity has passed to the evangelicals.

Thus we stand at this great moment of history. Tired of the unprecedented advance of secularism in twentieth-century society, we have attempted to cry out against it. When our cries were not heard, many of us retaliated with a political vengeance that made us a power with which to reckon. But what have we really accomplished?

WHAT HAVE WE ACCOMPLISHED?

The triumphalism of the Reagan landslides has subsided, leaving behind the stark realities of political life. In the aftermath of the Reagan revolution, little has changed regarding the social and moral issues which caused most Christians to get involved in politics in the first place. While this involvement brought many of these issues to the forefront of political debate, there has been little legislative correction that could not be undone by a different administration.[13]

While the New Right saw initial success in combating the Equal Rights Amendment and the Gay Rights movement, it failed to bring about any real significant change in regard to such issues as abortion on demand, public school prayer, and the teaching of creation in the public schools. Some progress has been made to stem the tide of pornography on both the local and national levels, and conservative justices have been appointed to every level of the judicial system, including the Supreme Court. However, many observers believe that the New Right has lost its momentum. Perhaps success came too quickly and too easily in 1980. Ronald Reagan won by a landslide, and many liberal politicians were voted out of office. While the degree of Christian impact on the election was debated, nearly everyone admitted that they had been a significant factor in sweeping a new administration into office.[14]

Intoxicated with their initial success, many conservatives were lulled into believing that they could change the political and social matrix of American culture overnight. Such presumption was a reflection of their naive understanding of how the political system actually works. They had confronted the system and won. Twentieth-century politics would never be the same. They had made a vital and lasting contribution to the political process by raising moral and social concerns to the forefront of political debate and by reaffirming our Judeo-Christian heritage.[15] However, unaccustomed to the rough-and-tumble arena of power politics and the need for compromise and negotiation, some became frustrated with the system. Others became alienated from the process altogether and chose to drop out.[16]

In time, the initial optimism faded and the early coalition began to fragment. Some began to call for more political involvement. Others were calling for less. Still others were saying, ''I told you we should never have gotten involved in the first place.'' The evangelical Christian community became confused and was left with a strange mixture of apathy and zealotry. Some have questioned whether the movement has lost momentum altogether.[17]

LOSS OF INTEGRITY

It has been said that the Christian ministry can be summed up in one word: integrity. Personal and spiritual integrity has always been an issue within the Church. As long as we kept our private religious beliefs and practices to ourselves, the world cared very little about us. But when preachers marched into the public arena, the public not only sat up and took notice, but they also demanded a greater accountability of us than we did of ourselves.

The public began asking questions which we should have been asking ourselves. They demanded a reasonable accounting of financial expenditures, fund-raising methods, and personal reimbursement. They questioned salaries, houses, and cars. The personal life-styles of Christian leaders became headline news across the country. The shocking revelations of the PTL sex and money scandal damaged the credibility of virtually all televangelists. The very people who had called for a moral revolution were now being called to task for moral failure by the secular press.[18]

Not only did this scandal affect televangelism in general, but it called into question the legitimacy of the very message of the Gospel—at least from the viewpoint of the secular world. It was the hottest news story of 1987, capturing the headlines for weeks at a time. The moral violations of this one ministry precipitated a wave of suspicion about all televangelists. Some secularists also made use of this lapse of integrity to discredit the entire Christian Right.[19]

For the first time in nearly a decade, the Christian Right was put on the defensive. Rather than attacking the moral failures of others, they were scrambling to defend their own integrity. Not only was society asking tough questions, but the public had turned cynical as well. Those who had lived by the media were now being crucified by it. While the scandal had little or nothing to do with their political involvement, it became the greatest potential blow to their political agenda. For the first time they had lost their public image of integrity. People wondered how televangelists could be trusted with the political destiny of others if they could not be trusted with the integrity of their own ministries.

LOSS OF VISION

Christians initially entered the political process with a clear sense of moral vision. They were tired of the incipient encroachment of secularism in nearly every area of American life. Their list of concerns included abortion, homosexuality, pornography, the breakdown of the traditional family, the exclusion of prayer from the public schools, and the general erosion of traditional values and public morality. They felt that the ship of state was in danger of running aground on the rocks of secularism. They even feared the eventual extinction of Judeo-Christian values.[20]

The perceived threat of secularism became the catalyst that bound together religiously and politically conservative people into a cohesive voting bloc. Like the fundamentalists of the early twentieth century who forged a coalition against theological liberalism, the New Right forged a coalition against political liberalism. The early successes of their political endeavors seduced many into thinking that political victories came easily. Enamored with their success and legitimized by the culture at large, they began to rest on their laurels. Some became so subsumed into the political process that they ceased to be a prophetic voice of correction. Since the Republican Party had adopted much of the agenda of the Religious Right, some religious leaders were hesitant to criticize the new administration.[21] In time, they were substantially neutralized and co-opted by the party. The clarity of their moral vision was clouded by political myopia.

LOSS OF MOMENTUM

Carl F. H. Henry, leading evangelical theologian, recently stated that the Religious Right had lost its momentum. In an interview in *Christianity Today,* he stated, "Diminished visibility is due in part to the fact that the New Right is no longer a media curiosity." He went on to observe that the sensationalism of the Religious Right has often worked against it. While complimenting their willingness to become involved in the political arena, Henry noted that many of their leaders are "naive about the political process." He also argued that the Religious Right lacks the cognitive force to counter the dominant secular and liberal ideology.[22]

The critics of the New Right have pointed to various signs of decline in the wishful hope that the entire movement has lost its momentum. They point to the restoration of the Democrats to the control of the Senate, the sagging popularity of Ronald Reagan, the Iran-Contra affair, the PTL scandal, Jerry Falwell's withdrawal from politics, and the theological conflict between fundamentalists and charismatics. However, Jeffrey Hadden, sociologist from the

University of Virginia and long-time critic of the New Right, believes that these estimations of demise are exaggerated. He states that the Religious Right is a "large constituency that no candidate can ignore." In the long run, he believes that they will shape the political process "more than it will shape them."[23]

Hadden then asks, "Why then this curiously pessimistic assessment from within what is rapidly becoming the most vigorous social-political movement in America?" He does not believe the answer is to be found in the various factors which are generally cited as evidence of the demise of the conservative agenda. Instead, he suggests, "The answer is to be found in the simple fact that many evangelical Christians have come to believe the negative stereotypes offered up by their critics." He observes that they are single-issue zealots who are quickly disillusioned when they don't win. While they can be mobilized for a single event, they often do not have the political savvy to effectively work the political system.[24]

Henry seems to be suggesting that there is an underlying apathy in the Religious Right that has neutralized its momentum, while Hadden seems to be suggesting that there is still an underlying current of zealotry within the Religious Right. It is the curious admixture of these two elements that characterizes evangelical political involvement at this time. On the one hand, there are those who are now implying that political involvement is antithetical to the true mission of the Church.[25] On the other hand, there are those who want to Christianize the political process by imposing a theocratic state.[26] Those caught in the middle between these two extremes of the continuum are often in a state of confusion.

THE CURRENT CONFUSION

There is no simple description of the current condition of the Religious Right. It is a whirlwind of ideologies, interests, and levels of commitment within a conservative context. No one person speaks for the entire movement. While certain leaders have been able to galvanize segments of the movement and rally them to specific issues, no one has ever been able to lead the entire movement consistently.

Indeed, many evangelicals are not at all comfortable with the agenda of the New Right or the Republican Party.[27] Others have become uncomfortable with the political process the longer they have been involved in it. Charles Colson's warnings reflect the concerns of many Christians who fear that the politicians may merely be using them to get their vote.[28]

This confusion has resulted in divided allegiances in response to the counter-signals being sent by evangelical leaders. Some seem to be urging more involvement, others want to get out of politics altogether, and still others appear to want to call "time out" and rethink the whole thing! There is a wide variety of reasons for these reactions. Initially, the leaders of the New Right were sincerely committed to their principles, but eventually some began to use the movement as a convenient means of raising funds and heightening their visibility. But whenever the press exposed the weaknesses or eccentricities of the movement, there were always detractors who quickly bailed out in an attempt to dissociate themselves from potential failure. Others overreacted to initial setbacks and began to question whether such involvement was worth it in the long run.

There were some leaders who became so heavily involved in political issues that their own ministries began to suffer neglect. They seemed incapable of drawing clear lines of demarcation between the ministry and politics. In time, many evangelical laymen tired of hearing constant sermonizing on political issues and became apathetic to the whole process. After all, their logic told them that the opposition had been neutralized, their man was in the White House—so why shouldn't they return to business as usual?

Oddly, on the other extreme, a number of religious activists arose calling for a Christian revolution that would use the democratic process to establish a theocratic state.[29] Under the rubric of "reconstructionism" or "Dominion theology," its proponents called for the rigid enforcement of Old Testament law and the Christianizing of American public education. Unfortunately, many of the critics of the New Right saw this as an expression of the sentiment of the entire evangelical community.[30]

DOES THE RELIGIOUS RIGHT HAVE A FUTURE?

In light of the current confusion, many critics are predicting the total demise of the Religious Right. Some feel that Pat Robertson's campaign may well have hindered the efforts of the New Right in the public arena. Even a casual study of the history of fundamentalist political involvement in the twentieth century indicates that whenever religious conservatives have faced defeat in the public domain, they have withdrawn from public life altogether. Sociologist James Davidson Hunter of the University of Virginia observes that there have been three waves of conservative political activism in the twentieth century:[31]

1. *Wave One*—1920s, Prohibition and anti-Catholic.
   This first wave of political activity was aimed at passing Prohibition legislation. It was also decidedly anti-Catholic. Billy Sunday was the folk hero and popular leader of this wave.
2. *Wave Two*—1950s, Anti-Communist.
   Led by Carl McIntire, this wave represented an evangelical response to the "Red Scare" of the McCarthy investigation into un-American activities.
3. *Wave Three*—1980s, Anti-Secularist.
   The third wave centered initially around Jerry Falwell and the Moral Majority, but it actually includes several diverse evangelical groups and leaders reacting against the secularization of American society.

In each of these waves of involvement, there was a heightened Christian commitment to political and social action.[32] There were also early victories and apparent successes which precipitated triumphalistic expectations. However, with each wave of activity an equally powerful counter-wave arose. In the aftermath of the repeal of Prohibition and the demise of the "Red Scare," Christians withdrew in embarrassment and frustration. While they significantly influenced public opinion, they failed to substantially change public policy. Some observers feel that the current wave of involvement is already beginning to subside in frustration and embarrassment. History may well be on the verge of repeating itself.

Despite the obvious parallels between the three waves, Hunter observes, "The political focus of conservative Protestant activism in this third wave was qualitatively different from anything preceding it in this century, but its complexion was markedly different too."[33] He notes that several factors had changed in the relationship of the evangelical and fundamentalist movement to society by the end of the twentieth century. According to survey data, the likelihood of evangelical political involvement has drastically shifted. Earlier surveys indicate that they were the least likely group to get involved, whereas current data indicate that they are now the most likely group to get involved. Another factor which Hunter points out is that the first two waves primarily involved single-focus issues, while the third wave was a response to the whole moral decline of Western culture.[34] It was more broadly focused and therefore appealed to broader segments of the population, including Catholics, Jews, Mormons, and even some conservative secularists.

Evangelical Christianity is at the crossroads. Having attained a window of opportunity at this moment in history, it is in danger of succumbing to the cycle of its own history. The time has come for clear thinking and decisive action. This is neither the time to overreact nor to withdraw.

The issues which precipitated conservative involvement are still the same. If they were important then, they are important now. The demographic studies clearly indicate that evangelicals are a large and growing segment of the American population.[35] We have the people that can make a difference in shaping and defining the American dream. Beneath our perceived divisions and apparent confusion, there remains an essentially concerned and informed population. The future is up to us!

Aleksandr Solzhenitsyn has said:

> If the world has not approached its end, it has reached a major watershed in history equal in importance to the turn from the Middle Ages to the Renaissance. It will demand from us a spiritual blaze; we shall have to rise to a new height of vision, to a new level of life, where our physical nature will not be crushed,

as in the Middle Ages, but even more importantly, our spiritual
being will not be trampled upon, as in the Modern Era.[36]

It is this sense of destiny which compels most evangelicals at the
present hour. It is obvious to virtually everyone that what has been
viewed as the traditional American culture is in danger of extinction. Whether this threat is real or perceived, it staggers the evangelical heart with the fear of a secularist future in which God,
religion, and religious values have no place.

Therefore, it is the threat of political power being used against
them that causes most evangelicals to want to influence or control
that power. We tend to be monarchists at heart, who think that if
"our" man is in control, then all will go well for us. Many of us
forget that our very entrance into politics may degenerate into the
use of force (*dunamis*) in the form of political coercion rather than
in the pursuit of spiritual power (*exousia*). Without spiritual authority, we cannot hope for much change through crass political power.

We who claim to trust in the sovereignty of God may at some
point have to put that trust to the ultimate test of faith. Just because
a professing Christian is running for office does not guarantee the
success of his endeavor. Nor does it necessarily mean that he or she
is the best candidate for the job. An individual may be a sincere
believer but an incompetent politician.

The Scriptures also remind us that there are times that God places
the worst of men into political power to accomplish His own goals
and purposes. In Daniel 4:17 we read, "The most High ruleth in the
kingdom of men, and giveth it to whomsoever he will, and setteth
up over it the basest of men." This in no way eliminates our
personal responsibility for influencing government any more than it
did for Daniel.

In fact, Scripture is filled with a wide variety of responses to politics
and governance. The judges, for the most part, were miserable
failures at human government. Saul lacked the character and skills of
leadership. David and Solomon were relatively successful rulers, but
each sowed the seeds of future destruction within his own administration. Most of the prophets had strong political opinions about their
rulers' personal lives and their administration of justice. Nathan,

Elijah, Elisha, Isaiah, and Jeremiah were directly involved in giving advice to political rulers. Daniel, Ezra, Nehemiah, and Esther also served in places of responsibility within hostile pagan governments.

By the time of Christ, people were divided over the issue of politics. The pious wanted to avoid all contamination of contact with Rome. The Herodians promoted total involvement, while the Pharisees and Sadducees preferred limited relations to further their own ends. On the other extreme, the Zealots wanted to overthrow the government by force and usher in the Messiah with an earthly kingdom.

Jesus stood above them all. Like a divine enigma on the landscape of humanity, He seemed to treat the political as mundane. When asked if He would pay the Roman tax, He asked to see the tribute coin. When it was produced, He asked, ''Whose is this image and superscription?'' (Matthew 22:20). When He was told it was Caesar's, He merely responded, ''Render therefore unto Caesar the things which are Caesar's; and unto God the things that are God's'' (Matthew 22:21).

Jesus always made it clear that the spiritual supersedes the political and that the political derives its authority from the spiritual. It is no wonder that He who was the embodiment of divine authority confounded His captors, accusers, and even the political governor who sentenced Him to die. ''I am innocent of the blood of this just person,'' Pilate protested, as he attempted to wash his hands of the whole matter. But no one has ever believed that excuse, and indeed we should not, for the Bible clearly teaches that we are our brother's keeper, and responsible under God for the governance of human affairs.

When Jesus gave the Great Commission to His disciples to evangelize the world, He said ''All power [Greek, *exousia*] is given unto me in heaven and in earth'' (Matthew 28:18). It is on the basis of that divine authority that He commissions us to be His representatives here on earth. As such, we can neither abdicate the sociopolitical consequences of discipleship, as did the medieval monastics, nor can we hope to bring about His Kingdom on earth by the mere use of political or legal force. Therein lies the tension between religion and politics, and therein must come the solution.

Chapter Three

The New Right Emerges: Ready—Fire—Aim

Blessed are ye, when men shall revile you, and persecute you, and shall say all manner of evil against you. . . .

Matthew 5:11

 The recent resurgence of conservative Christian involvement in the social and political life of America is the religious phenomenon of our time. It has become the most heatedly discussed religious issue of the 1980s.[1] With the founding of the Moral Majority in 1979, fundamentalists ventured into the political process. They were not welcomed with open arms by the political or religious establishments. Rather, they kicked down the door and marched in with such force that they sent panic and paranoia through most sectors of American society.

The media were shocked. Where did all these fundamentalists come from? Who were they and what did they want? Since the general public had assumed that fundamentalists disappeared after the Scopes Trial in 1925, they were at a loss to explain their sudden public resurgence. A kind of "Fundomania" set in, and some began to assert that hordes of bigoted Bible-bangers had formed a conspiracy to take over America and set up a theocratic dictatorship.[2] Since then, responsible analysis has shown "Fundomania" to be a myth provoked mainly by media exaggeration.[3]

During the 1980 presidential campaign, rhetoric was running high on every side. Church historian Martin Marty warned, "Before 1980 ends, not a few candidates will have ducked for cover to escape the Fundamentalist barrage."[4] Gary Jarmin of Christian Voice announced, "We have targeted about thirty-five members of Congress and the Senate . . . whom we think we can retire from Congress in November."[5] Former Southern Baptist president Reverend Jimmy Allen denounced the "total capitulation of a segment of the evangelical Christian movement to right-wing politics and sword-rattling jingoism."[6] The liberal intellectual elite compared the New Right to "Islamic fundamentalism" and Jerry Falwell to the Ayatollah Khomeini. One author went so far as to describe fundamentalists by stating, "He is coming after you to get you to join his army. If you don't want to join, he's coming after you anyway."[7]

Today most of the rhetoric has subsided, but there is still an underlying uneasiness about fundamentalist involvement in the political process. As Pat Robertson's bid for the presidency indicated, the issue of religion and politics will not go away. His candidacy brought Christian political involvement to a precarious moment in history. If the balance between religion and politics can be further advanced, then candidacies such as Robertson's will prove beneficial to the American democratic process. However, if the result is a polarized American society, the avenue of religious involvement in politics may well be lost.

A HISTORICAL OVERVIEW

Any legitimate assessment of the evangelical-fundamentalist involvement in American politics must be viewed in its historical and social context. Conservative Christians are as old as the Church itself. They have worn different labels at different times in history, but they have always been there.[8] By the end of the nineteenth century, conservative Protestants were generally known as "evangelicals."[9] They merged two opposing theological strains: Calvinistic Puritanism and Wesleyan Revivalism. As the twentieth century dawned, they also became increasingly premillennial and dispensational in their eschatology.[10]

Most historians agree that conservative Protestants were not generally politically active as a body during the nineteenth century, despite the controversy over slavery that evoked a great deal of civil religious rhetoric on both sides of the issue. However, as the twentieth century dawned, the evangelical movement was confronted with the threat of theological liberalism. The reaction within the evangelical wing of American Protestantism produced the Fundamentalist Controversy (1909–1929).

Theological Controversy

As early as 1909, several evangelical scholars began producing a series of booklets known as *The Fundamentals* and hence the name of a movement was born.[11] Essentially fundamentalism was a doctrinal controversy centering upon the essential (fundamental) elements of Christian theology. These were generally articulated as (1) the inspiration of Scripture, (2) deity and virgin birth of Christ, (3) His substitutionary atonement, (4) His literal resurrection, and (5) His literal second coming.[12]

University of Virginia sociologist James D. Hunter has shown that the appeal of fundamentalist theology was consistent with the popular culture of the time.[13] Therefore, fundamentalism has enjoyed massive appeal to working-class middle America throughout most of the twentieth century. While evangelical and fundamentalist churches have grown remarkably during this century, the more liberal mainline denominations have declined drastically.[14] During the decade of the 1970s, the United Methodists lost nearly a million members and the Episcopal Church lost a half-million. In the past twenty years, mainline denominations have experienced a combined membership decline of nearly 5 million people.[15]

In its September 2, 1985, issue, *Time* magazine heralded the growth of fundamentalism with a cover feature and two editorials on the impact of conservative Christianity in America. Noting that fundamentalists "have not been so well financed, visible, organized and effective" since the 1920s, the editorials acknowledged that fundamentalism is "bursting beyond the church walls into the wider society."[16] In an era of theological indifference and ethical relativism, fundamentalism has become a predominant voice in our nation's public policies.

Political Involvement

The alliance between Protestant orthodoxy and political conservatism has long been recognized. One observer has called it an "idealized vision of the American identity and experience."[17] On the other hand, Lutheran theologian Richard Neuhaus told New York's Harvard Club, "I believe the New Religious Right is a long-term phenomenon in American life. These people must be engaged as partners in the process of redefining America."[18] *Newsweek* recently said: "What is clear both on the philosophical level—and in the rough-and-tumble arena of politics—is that the Falwells of the nation and their increasingly militant and devoted flocks are a phenomenon that can no longer be dismissed or ignored."[19]

Evangelical and fundamentalist political activism has reached three major peaks in the twentieth century: (1) the anti-Catholic wave of the 1920s, which included antievolutionary and protemperance elements; (2) the anticommunist wave of the 1950s, which hitchhiked onto the McCarthy "Red Scare"; (3) the antisecularist wave of the 1980s, which is attempting to stem the tide of moral decline in American culture.[20]

In each of these peaks of political activism, fundamentalists have been labeled as ultraconservative, bigoted, intolerant, and absolutist fanatics.[21] Yet in each case they had strong populist appeal representing a grass-roots, antielitist movement. Also, in each case public reaction against them has always come from the political left.

Social Assessment

The social and cultural matrix of American fundamentalism has generally been described as a white, middle-class working community. However, this mix is changing drastically today as evangelicals and fundamentalists become more educated and upwardly mobile in society. In other words, we are now seeing the development of an evangelical "yuppie" community.[22] Traditional stereotypes often do not apply any longer. Recent studies have shown that the moral issues of the New Right are supported by groups as diverse as working-class blacks and college-educated whites. The numerical success of such groups as Bev LaHaye's Concerned

Women for America reveals that a more significant number of females are involved in the political right than ever before.

The current coalition of the New Right includes television evangelists, direct mail fund-raisers and conservative politicians. But it also reflects a grass roots concern over basic threats to traditional family and moral values. Threats such as alcohol, drugs, television, violence, pornography, homosexuality, and abortion had galvanized a great segment of American society into a political backlash against the policies of the Democratic Party in general and the Carter administration in particular.[23]

The first attempts to mobilize televangelists for political purposes came in 1976 under the encouragement of Richard Viguerie and Paul Weyrich. During the campaign, a few trial runs were made at direct mail fund-raising with inconclusive results. However, the controversy over Jimmy Carter's interview with *Playboy* magazine triggered a hostile reaction from Jerry Falwell on his "Old-Time Gospel Hour" broadcast, and the war was on between Falwell and Carter.[24]

THE REAGAN YEARS

The high tide of conservative religious involvement in American politics came during the presidential campaigns of 1980 and 1984, when Ronald Reagan won landslide victories over Jimmy Carter and Walter Mondale. During the 1980 campaign, fundamentalists surged back into the political arena for the first time since the repeal of Prohibition nearly fifty years earlier. Upset with the liberal drift to the left both politically and theologically, and disturbed by the "moral shock" of the 1970s, conservative Christians began to form an alliance of cobelligerency for self-defense. Just as the common threat of liberalism rallied the early fundamentalists together in the 1920s, so now the common threat of secularism and humanism brought together an unusual coalition of fundamentalists, evangelicals, and even charismatics.[25]

While the formation of this religiously conservative coalition may still mystify some, to its adherents it was a matter of self-preservation. They viewed themselves as being threatened by the secularization of society. Upset by the Supreme Court decisions to ban prayer in the public schools and to allow abortion on demand, these conservatives reacted to reverse the trend of the time.

Birth of the Moral Majority

One specific reaction to the increasing secularization of American society was the formation of the Moral Majority in 1979. With the assistance of James Kennedy, Charles Stanley, Tim LaHaye, and others, Jerry Falwell formed a nonpartisan political organization to promote morality in public life. The Moral Majority took its name from Richard Nixon's earlier use of the term "silent majority." The organization was not limited to fundamentalist Christians, but included Catholics, Jews, and Mormons who shared similar moral convictions.[26]

In time, this new political cooperation was severely criticized. The political left branded it manipulative power politics that smacked of McCarthyism. On the other hand, the religious right maligned Falwell for promoting religious ecumenism under the guise of political cooperation.[27] Falwell was called the "most dangerous man in America" by fellow fundamentalists. Interestingly, evangelical theologian Carl F. H. Henry predicted this reaction many years earlier when he wrote, "There are fundamentalists who will insist immediately that no evangelical has the right to unite with non-evangelicals in any reform."[28]

Before the year was over, however, Falwell and others had rallied a large segment of the conservative Christian community through a combination of mass rallies, television specials, and direct mail appeals. The new conservatives mobilized millions of previously inactive voters to make their beliefs count at the ballot box. Sensing an impending moral crisis, various groups were formed to combat any further legislation that could be viewed as detrimental to Christian churches, schools, and families.[29] Rather than trying to "take over" America, the New Rightists were trying to protect themselves from being taken over by a secular society.

"A New Beginning"

The slogan for the 1980 Republican Convention held in Detroit was "A New Beginning." In the candidacy of Ronald Reagan, conservatives found the ray of hope for which they had been waiting for fifty years. Ironically, Reagan himself has remained detached from organized religion. The New Right overlooked his divorce and the fact that his own personal faith was somewhat vague. He was their champion because he championed the ideals which they believed in so strongly.

Several loosely structured conservative organizations lined up with Reagan. These included Christian Voice, the Religious Roundtable, the National Christian Action Coalition, and several right-to-life groups. One of their unique early strategies was the establishment of target lists and moral report cards.[30] Though these methods were widely criticized, the New Right was eventually successful in helping defeat Senators George McGovern of South Dakota, Frank Church of Idaho, John Culver of Iowa, Birch Bayh of Indiana, and Gaylord Nelson of Wisconsin. Of the targeted senators, only Alan Cranston of California survived.

Ironically, TV evangelist Pat Robertson stayed clear of any involvement with Moral Majority and eventually resigned from the Religious Roundtable because it had become "too political."[31] Nevertheless, his enthusiasm for the themes of the New Right was unmistakable. The same was true of Jim Bakker, then host of the "PTL Club."[32]

Leadership of the New Right fell almost totally to Jerry Falwell, a Baptist fundamentalist. Falwell himself admitted: "As a pastor, I kept waiting for someone to come to the forefront of the American religious scene to lead the way out of the wilderness. Like thousands of other preachers, I kept waiting, but no real leader appeared. Finally, I realized that we had to act ourselves. Something had to be done now."[33] Citing his disgust with the legalization of abortion, threats to the traditional family, rising sentiment toward so-called homosexual rights, and the Equal Rights Amendment, Falwell committed himself to lead a religious campaign which he called "a return to moral sanity."

Moral Majority's support for the Reagan candidacy and the Republican platform soon became synonymous. Hill and Owen have observed, "What Moral Majority did then, was to galvanize incipient organizations and provide them with a way to achieve some self-identity and cohesiveness, as well as enable them to move from a position of alienation to center stage in the national political drama."[34]

"Washington for Jesus"

As the New Right began to gain momentum, the Reverend John Gimenez of Virginia Beach organized a "Washington for Jesus" rally on April 29, 1980, at the Capitol mall. Pat Robertson and Bill Bright of Campus Crusade were named as cochairmen. An impressive crowd in excess of 200,000 turned out for the rally. The audience was predominantly charismatic, and Falwell was noticeably absent.

The importance of the rally was that the national media interpreted it as a political demonstration.[35] It thereby helped publicize the numerical clout of the New Right, which was now, in Erling Jorstad's words, "fully in public view."[36] Though the rally was condemned by the National Council of Churches, it only encouraged the New Right to bolder action. The public visibility of the television preachers was perceived as a statement of support for the Reagan candidacy, and indeed it was.

Dallas Rally

In early 1980 the polls showed Carter still the favorite among the evangelical-fundamentalist bloc. But by mid-summer they had swung almost totally to Reagan. A key turning point came in August, when James Robison and Ed McAteer of the Religious Roundtable organized 20,000 people in a rally in Dallas, Texas. The three major candidates were invited to speak. Carter and Anderson refused; Reagan accepted.

In his address, Reagan said, "If we believe God has blessed America with liberty, then we have not just a right to vote, but a duty to vote." He promised to keep government out of the churches, schools, and homes. He applauded "old-time religion." Then came the magic moment when he brought the delegates to their feet in joyous approval. "I know you can't endorse me," Reagan said, "but I want you to know that I endorse you."[37] His statement electrified the crowd, giving them the approval they had so long

50

sought. No longer were they a tangential element of society; they were recognized and accepted by the man who would be the next president of the United States.

Victory in 1980

The Reagan-Bush landslide victory proved that the New Right was here to stay. While their real influence in the election may be debated, one fact was clear: The New Right had not been repudiated at the polls. The Republican victory brought in twelve new senators and the first Senate majority for the Republicans in twenty-six years. While the Democrats retained control of the House of Representatives, they lost thirty-two seats to the Republicans. Even more significantly, fourteen of the fifteen senatorial candidates backed by the Moral Majority were victorious.

Optimism and euphoria were running high. Falwell announced, "We now have a Washington government that will help us."[38] Jarmin of Christian Voice said, "It's the beginning of a new era of conservatism in America." Pat Robertson was ecstatic and began to show a greater interest in New Right politics. Direct mail fund-raisers like Viguerie began planning strategies for the 1982 and 1984 elections. Reagan and Bush openly praised the efforts of Falwell and Moral Majority.[39]

Reality Sets In: Success and Failure

In the four years between the presidential campaigns, the New Right continued its efforts to lobby Congress and register new voters. According to various reports, by 1981 the New Right groups had enlisted 70,000 clergy and had registered 4 to 5 million voters.[40] During those four years, a conservative mood settled over the country. The Republican platform took a conservative posture toward such issues as abortion, the Equal Rights Amendment, homosexuality, and school prayer. The largest segments of the evangelical-fundamentalist community already held these sentiments and lined up behind the Republican administration. Political activism by religious conservatives was not only tolerated, but encouraged.

By 1984, however, the harsh realities of politics had set in. Efforts to change federal law to allow voluntary prayer in the public schools failed. However, legislation allowing religious groups to use public school facilities was passed. Legislative efforts to require the teaching of scientific creationism along with evolution in the public schools were relatively unsuccessful. Pro-life groups also failed to achieve their ultimate goal of an amendment outlawing abortion.

Despite setbacks, there were also noticeable successes. Efforts to pass Gay Rights legislation were successfully blocked in the early 1980s. The Equal Rights Amendment was defeated and all subsequent efforts to revive it have been futile. Federal funding for abortions was prohibited by the Supreme Court's upholding of the Hyde Amendment.

James Hunter has observed that the media attention the New Right created over its agenda was a victory in itself.[41] Even groups like People for the American Way that mobilized against the New Right were relatively unsuccessful. Extremist propaganda like Conway and Siegelman's *Holy Terror* was also dismissed as irrelevant.[42] "Fundomania" began to die out and the New Right was accepted as a legitimate part of the political process.

Richard Neuhaus, a main line conservative, published his landmark study entitled *The Naked Public Square,* in which he appealed for religious thinkers to influence public opinion with religious and moral values and thus shape the vision of America. To fail to do so, he argued, would leave the square of public opinion naked of religious values and vulnerable to antireligious secularism.[43] A similar theme was advocated by the late Francis Schaeffer in his monumental work, *The Christian Manifesto*. He too called for active religious involvement in American public life. He argued that failure to do so would abdicate to a totally secular world view based on the final reality of impersonal matter and energy shaped by impersonal chance.[44]

Victory in 1984

By the time Ronald Reagan defeated Walter Mondale in the 1984 election, evangelical public opinion had been galvanized behind the Republican ticket. However, as in all second-term victories, there was no landslide effect in the House or Senate. It was obvious that the televangelists accepted the inevitability of Reagan's reelection and campaigned less fervently than they had in 1980. This time there were no report cards or target lists. Indeed, the civilizing of the New Right was already taking place.

In a very real sense, evangelicalism had been spoiled by its own success, as at least one writer had earlier warned.[45] A mood of apathy began to set in. Times were good, the economy was strong, and what was even more important, the evangelical-fundamentalist community no longer felt threatened. The two most influential vice-presidents of the Moral Majority, Ron Godwin and Cal Thomas, both resigned in 1985 to pursue careers in the secular press. Jerry Falwell himself announced that he was getting out of politics in 1986 and "going back to the basics" of his ministry. Yet at the same time Pat Robertson, who had stayed out of the earlier campaigns, announced his candidacy for the Republican nomination for president in 1988.

Evangelicalism had now come full cycle in ten years. In 1976, Jimmy Carter was elected president despite his claim to be a born again Christian. In 1980, thousands of "born again" preachers rallied to put Carter out of office in favor of the religiously vague Ronald Reagan, who was more committed to their political agenda. Finally, Robertson believed the only way to fully realize that agenda was for a preacher to become president.[46] The cycle had worked like this: (1) It is acceptable for a Christian to be in politics, even to become president; (2) it is acceptable for preachers themselves to influence the political process; (3) it is desirable for a preacher to become president.

Robertson's presidential bid was certainly damaged by the crisis among televangelists brought on by Oral Roberts's extremist fund-raising tactics and the controversy surrounding Jim Bakker and the PTL Network. Several crucial questions need to be answered: Where does all of this leave us? How involved should we be in politics? Is politics even the answer to our dilemma? Has our limited success been worth the effort we have put forth? Where do we go from here?

WHAT HAVE WE LEARNED?

The old adage that people never learn from history is frighteningly true. This is certainly the case with the current evangelical involvement with politics. Before we can even begin to assess where we go from here, several observations need to be clarified. All too often the reactionary philosophy of the New Right has been one of ready-fire-aim! We are so quick to attack what we oppose that we often lose sight of our true objectives.

Our approach to religio-political issues may be categorized in these four ways:

1. Preservationist. One of our ultimate goals is to preserve our own beliefs and way of life. We often feel threatened by the changing world around us. We fear that the gradual secularization of society will replace religion with an antireligious, antagonistic secularism. We foresee a society cut off from its religious heritage adrift on the intellectual sea of moral neutrality. These fears are real and certainly based upon solid facts.[47] The ideological assault on religion is evident in secular literature all the way down to the level of school textbooks and popular novels.

One glaring criticism, however, of our preservationist mentality is that it is often self-centered and promotes only self-interest. We lack a comprehensive philosophy of social justice that extends to the needs of others. Issues such as poverty, racial justice, world hunger, and economic inequities are given occasional lip service, but rarely acted upon by the New Right. Even in regard to the issue of international peace, our only solution seems to be that of increased military armament.

If we are to be taken seriously by politicians and the general public, we must develop a comprehensive moral and social philosophy that extends beyond our own self-interest. At the same time, it must be practically implemented within our political structure.

2. Reactionary. Conservatives have long been accused of being reactionary in their politics. We are generally known for what we are against more than what we are for. Our objectionist mentality tends to defend the status quo and oppose new solutions to old problems. And often we are right. Our opposition helps keep society from running in the direction of social nihilism.

However, there is a glaring weakness with reactionary politics. It excels in condemning other proposals while offering none of its own. We are quick to express our criticism of the government while failing to correct it. We love to curse the darkness, but often forget to light a candle of positive action. For years we were never taken seriously because we offered no real political alternatives. We were content to complain about government in private but had little to offer in the way of public action.

Another weakness of reactionary politics is our inability to establish unified action on a given issue. We are still struggling with the abortion issue because we are divided among ourselves on how the argument should be framed. In the give-and-take of the political process, a great deal of negotiation and compromise are necessary. However, some are unwilling to make any compromises and thus are incapable of working effectively within the American political structure. On the other hand, our very involvement in the process tends to neutralize our position and may make us less effective in the long run.

3. Populist. Conservatives tend to gravitate to populist, grass roots movements. The New Right is certainly such a movement involving the mobilization of middle- and lower-class Americans into the political life of our nation. As a group, we often lack the intellectual base and political savvy to accomplish our goals. We tend to have a simplistic mentality about the power of the president. We think that if we can elect "our man" to the White House, he alone can solve all of our problems. We have totally neglected other levels of political office in recent elections.

We cannot bring about permanent change at the executive level alone. We must influence the entire legislative system. To our credit, we began doing that in 1980, but since then we have failed miserably. In some cases we have been unsuccessful at the level of city government, let alone Congress.

If the New Right is to succeed in extending its influence beyond the Reagan presidency, we must develop the kind of thinking that moves beyond public approval and promotes what we believe to be right, whether it is popular or not.

4. Pragmatic. Unlike so-called evangelical "centrists" whose proposals have often been categorized as intellectual idealism, we tend to be very pragmatic in our approach to power politics.[48] To our credit, we have learned how to make the system work on our behalf. We know how to register voters and rally them behind an issue or a candidate. However, our greatest success is in keeping the other guy *out* of office, rather than getting our guy *in* office. We virtually paint the opponent as the antichrist in order to keep our people from voting for him.

However, in many cases, our people don't know the real issues of the campaign. They just know that the "Christian thing" to do is to vote for so-and-so. We must help our constituency to be more informed on the issues themselves. Further, we must be careful not to use an issue merely to raise money. Some issues provoke a better response than others. Therefore, there is a tendency to avoid those that don't raise money and to stress those that do. If we are not cautious, we could pragmatically shift our attention away from an important but unpopular issue and toward an insignificant issue that generates a lot of financial support. This is an especially dangerous tendency among direct mail fund-raisers who are always looking for a "hot button" to push.[49]

A PHILOSOPHY OF CHRISTIAN POLITICAL INVOLVEMENT

This emphasizes the need to establish a clearly defined philosophy of Christian political involvement which would include several key factors:

1. Theological and Philosophical Basis. If we are going to seriously affect American political and social life, we must understand what it is we are trying to accomplish. We are not merely advocating the election of certain officials as an end in itself. Francis Schaeffer clearly understood this when he argued that Christ must be Lord in all of life. He wrote, "He is our Lord not just in religious things and not just in cultural things . . . but in our intellectual lives, and in business, and in our relation to society, and in our attitude toward the moral breakdown of our culture."[50] Acknowledging His Lordship involves placing ourselves under the authority of Scripture and thinking and acting as citizens of His Kingdom as well as citizens of earth.

It is in this regard that the Christian understands that the wrongs of society are not merely social ills, but spiritual ills. As such, they require spiritual help, not merely political readjustment. Ultimately, there are no permanent political solutions to the problems of society. But that does not mean that we should all retreat to a monastery and advocate social anarchy for the rest of the world.

Because the Christian is a citizen of two kingdoms—one earthly, the other heavenly—he has an obligation to both. He cannot divorce himself from either or both. He is under divine mandate to both. Nevertheless, he realizes that the one is temporal and the other eternal. But that in no way prohibits his involvement in the temporal; in fact, it enhances it. The Christian cannot merely sit by and passively watch society self-destruct. Something within him, namely the Spirit of God, cries out for truth and justice. Wherever the cry has been articulated into action, truth and justice have prevailed.

2. Long-Range Strategy. There are no instant solutions to complex problems. The New Right has often been criticized for offering simple answers to complex questions. However, this need not be the case. We do have valuable answers to the really important issues of the day, and those answers need to be articulated clearly and thoughtfully. This is not the time for arrogance or overstatement of our case. Neither is this the time for capitulation. No one ever said this process would be easy! Those who naively thought Ronald Reagan would solve all the ills of American society by himself have been gravely disappointed. On the other hand, conditions have improved so that religious conservatives have been able to make their voices heard in a way that was not possible prior to 1980.

One of our greatest needs today is for a long-range strategy to enact our goals and objectives. We cannot rest on the laurels of the past or the future will catch us unprepared. Serious questions need to be addressed now: Where do we go after Reagan? What if the next president is more hostile to our agenda? Do we give up or do we dig in deeper?

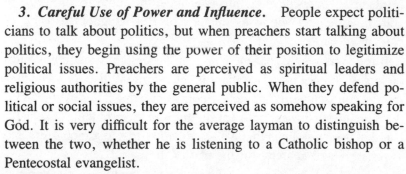

3. Careful Use of Power and Influence. People expect politicians to talk about politics, but when preachers start talking about politics, they begin using the power of their position to legitimize political issues. Preachers are perceived as spiritual leaders and religious authorities by the general public. When they defend political or social issues, they are perceived as somehow speaking for God. It is very difficult for the average layman to distinguish between the two, whether he is listening to a Catholic bishop or a Pentecostal evangelist.

The particular power of televangelists is that they are the only preachers some people listen to, since they rarely attend a local church. Therefore, they are greatly influenced by them. Many of these viewers lack the spiritual discernment to properly evaluate what they are hearing. Therefore, we must be very cautious in the statements we make regarding religion and politics.

Caution must also be exercised in regard to those with whom we disagree. When preachers start talking about politics, it becomes very tempting to label our opponents as the "devil" and their views as "antichristian."[51] Unfortunately, this has been the case throughout most of Church history. In some cases, our political opponents will even be fellow believers who need to be respected as such, even though we may seriously disagree on political matters.

This is perhaps the most difficult issue of all for Christians in politics. We are all so quick to believe that "God is on our side" that we tend to see our political opponents as God-hating, Christ-denying hypocrites. Unfortunately, this kind of prejudice works both ways and has been used *on* the New Right as well as *by* the New Right.

4. Financial Integrity and Accountability. Certainly the misuse of funds uncovered during the PTL scandal serves as a reminder to every ministry that integrity in fund-raising and accountability in financial expenditures is essential. We must not become deceived by the tyranny of the urgent and lose sight of our ultimate objectives.

Some preachers have found politics to be a great potential fund-raiser and have lost sight of why they are raising funds in the first place. Socio-political issues are not important because they raise money, but because they touch upon matters of eternal truth.

It is also true that some issues raise money better than others. Preachers need to be especially careful that they do not focus only on those issues that are financially profitable, but on issues of truth, whether they are popular or not and whether they produce funds or not. Defending the rights of the unborn, for example, may not be lucrative, but this is certainly one of the great issues of our time.

5. The Priority of Justice. According to Scripture, the ultimate authority of law comes from God and is a reflection of His nature and character. In this sense even majority rule is not always right. Paul Marshall of the Institute of Christian Studies in Toronto, Canada, has correctly recognized, "At times even constitutional limits are not sufficient and great injustice can still be done even while following constitutional rules."[52] He cites the case of Hitler, who was supported by a large majority of Germans and was able to function within legal parameters while slaughtering millions of innocent people.

At times the greater issues of human justice transcend political boundaries. The real issue today is not whether one is a Democrat or a Republican, but whether he is committed to justice for people. This means that we must defend the rights of those with whom we disagree. Suppressing their freedoms in the name of religion is just as wrong as for them to suppress ours. We are only asking for the opportunity to be heard in the debate on public policy. Now that we have everyone's attention, we need to think carefully about what we are going to say.

SUMMARY

Christians are, in the words of Jesus, "in the world," but "not of the world" (see John 17:11–16). We are caught in a divinely intended tension between the temporal and the eternal. As citizens of earth and in particular of earthly governments, we cannot be apolitical or uninvolved. We are already involved by virtue of living in God's world. We cannot sit by and do nothing while ignorance and injustice prevail. The Spirit of God within us cries out against all such indifference. We must be involved in society in order to reach society for Jesus Christ.

At the same time, we also recognize that political solutions are temporary at best. Legislation alone cannot produce a just and moral society apart from the regenerating work of God in the hearts of men. We, more than anyone, must point society beyond the temporal to the eternal. We must never lose sight of who we really are and why we are here. Our Christianity must make a difference in the world in which we live. Maintaining justice is a corporate responsibility of the Body of Christ. Theological differences may divide us ecclesiastically, and even at times politically, but they must not obscure our unified witness to Christ as the Lord of all of life.

In the Old Testament when Joshua was preparing to cross the Jordan into the promised land, he met a man with his sword drawn against him. As commander of the army of Israel, he boldly demanded, "Are you for us or for our enemies?" The Captain of the army of the Lord replied, "Neither!" He then went on to explain that He was on God's side and demanded that Joshua acknowledge His sovereignty above his own (*see* Joshua 5:13–15).

There can be little doubt that the Captain of the Lord's army was Christ Himself. His earthly name Jesus is the equivalent to the Old Testament name Joshua; both mean "savior." In essence, "a savior" Joshua, had met "*the* Savior," Jesus, and surrendered to His Lordship and authority before ever attempting to carry out God's plan for social justice in the promised land. We, too, are at best little "saviors," doing all we can under the authority of the Savior to proclaim truth and justice to our social order. May we never lose sight of the fact that He alone is Lord.

Chapter Four

The Bible and Politics: Do They Mix?

Sanctify them through thy truth: thy word is truth.
John 17:17

 When fundamentalists became involved in the political arena in 1980, they not only shocked the general public, but they stunned a lot of other Christians as well. Were these the same people who had dismissed the evangelical call for social action in the 1950s as irrelevant? Were they the same group that rejected the civil rights movement of the 1960s as dangerous? Religious conservatives, who had abstained from social and political involvement since the repeal of Prohibition, were now intoxicated with political fervor. What precipitated the change?

Unfortunately, it was *not* a new understanding of biblical truth. While they were certainly influenced by their scriptural beliefs, it was the pressure of external forces that provoked fundamentalists into a new posture of social concern and political action. Just as fundamentalists had forged a loosely knit coalition against the threat of theological liberalism in the early part of the century, so now they forged a new coalition against the threat of secularism in the culture at large.[1]

Since this new coalition represented divergent groups of fundamentalists, evangelicals, and charismatics, it did not represent a consistent theology. Some were angry with society in general.

61

Others were upset with the Democrats in particular. Still others had broader social and moral concerns. Some saw it as an opportunity to protest the trend toward secularization, and others saw it as an opportunity to establish a Christian political alternative.[2]

In reality, many issues prompted this conservative political reaction from the conservative religious community. While right wing theology and right wing politics do not inevitably go hand in hand, they often do. Political action is, in reality, an extension of one's personal beliefs into society.[3] Politics are never purely neutral. They are legal extensions of morality and belief systems, whatever those systems may be. The fundamentalist reaction against Jimmy Carter was not a reaction against him personally, but against the perceived political beliefs and practices of the Democratic Party.

In such issues as legalized abortion, pornography, homosexuality, feminism, and the encroachment of the federal government into church and Christian school affairs, fundamentalists perceived the growth of an evolving secularism which threatened the existence of Judeo-Christian values.[4] That perception was not without foundation. Evangelical theologian Francis Schaeffer warned, "Evangelical accommodation to the world of our age represents the removal of the last barrier against the breakdown of our culture."[5] While the validity of this "last barrier" mentality may be debated, it was this concept which provoked fundamentalists and evangelicals to act without first devising a theological justification for their action.[6]

One specific reaction to the secularization of American life was the founding of the Moral Majority in 1979 by Jerry Falwell, James Kennedy, Charles Stanley, Tim LaHaye, and Greg Dixon.[7] They established a nonpartisan political organization to promote morality in public life. Moral Majority was not a religious organization, though its ideology was significantly shaped by fundamentalist theology. In time the new organization included Catholics, Jews, and Mormons, as well as fundamentalist and evangelical Protestants. The underlying methodology was that of cobelligerency, which had been advocated by the late Francis Schaeffer and even earlier by Carl F. H. Henry.[8] While this newfound political cooperation was criticized by some as a kind of religious ecumenicalism, it proved very effective in giving the New Right the appearance of influence beyond its own constituency.

The political positions of the New Right have been easily identified by friend and foe alike. However, the theological presuppositions that support those political positions are infinitely more difficult to identify.[9] The involvement of the New Right was so reactionary that it functioned on the level of power politics and rarely dealt with theoretical issues. Therefore, it was often accused of promoting a "crusading moralism" under the guise of "civil religion."[10] One writer has warned, "When we are convinced that what we are doing is identical with the kingdom of God, anyone who opposes us must be wrong. . . . But when this mentality possesses us, we are taking the power of God and using it for our own needs."[11]

BIBLICAL MANDATE FOR POLITICAL INVOLVEMENT

For many years fundamentalists subscribed to a dichotomous worldview that magnified the sacred and minimized the secular. Since social and political issues were categorized as secular pursuits, they were deemed secondary to the priority of world evangelization. In fact, some fundamentalists believed that true Christians should abstain from all such secular activity.

This call to withdraw from society was nothing new. Early Christian hermits were experts at it. They lived in isolation from the world and from each other. Later, monasticism became a communal collection of hermits relating to one another but not to the world around them. In American society, the Amish and Old Order Mennonites developed their own communities isolated from modern society. The one great limitation of this approach is that it rarely influences the rest of society.

The Church and Society

Throughout Church history, five basic church and society models have been proposed.[12]

1. Isolation. This approach advocates a total or near-total isolation of Christians from society. It urges believers to live in relation to God alone and it isolates the Church from any social or political action. Pietistic fundamentalism has a tendency in this direction. It adopts the attitude, "If we forget about the world, it won't bother us."

2. Accommodation.   This approach encourages the Church to accommodate itself to society in order to influence it. This has been the general approach of Protestant liberalism. It seeks its identification within society. On the one hand, it avoids the extreme of isolation, but on the other hand, it generally succumbs to a capitulation of its values to those of the secular society.

3. Condemnation.   This is the position of many militant fundamentalists, who are quick to condemn the ills of society while offering little or nothing to correct them. They know what they don't like but are never really clear about what to do about it. While many aspects of society need to be confronted by the Church, society also needs the opportunity to establish proper alternatives which are biblically based.

4. Integration.   According to this approach, there is always a tension between the Church and society which reflects what Luther called the "eschatological struggle between the power of God and the powers of evil."[13] In this model, which has generally been adopted by the evangelical community, the Christian has a constructive role to play in society. Therefore, he may influence society by his presence, but he generally does so with little or no intention of changing society by social or political action.

5. Transformation.   This is the model developed by John Calvin, who believed God was sovereign both over the Church and the State. He saw the Church as involved in the ceaseless activity of bringing order out of chaos. In the political realm, this means transforming society by the authority of Scripture and under the claims of the Lordship of Christ. He wrote that government should "adopt our conduct to human society, to form our manners to civil justice, to conciliate us to each other, and to cherish common peace and tranquility."[14] He viewed public magistrates as ordained servants of God to protect innocence, modesty, honor, and tranquility.

We believe that the transformation model is the most biblically correct. It takes seriously the commands of Christ to influence society and evangelize the world. It also recognizes the unique authority of Scripture in defining culture. As the Word of God, the Bible judges human culture. It is not merely a product of that culture. If Scripture is true, then it must be obeyed and that obedience often involves a confrontation with what is wrong in society.

The Bible and Freedom

In both the Old and New Testaments there is a direct relationship between the proclamation of God's redemptive purpose and social concern. The Bible promises individual and national blessing to those who conform to God's laws and warns of both individual and national judgment for those who violate them. All the Old Testament prophets proclaim a message of corporate responsibility. God's people were called upon to care for the poor, promote social justice, deliver the oppressed, and defend the defenseless.[15]

Nowhere does the New Testament contradict the social concern of the Old Testament prophets. Rather, it emphasizes that the ultimate transformation of society can only come through acknowledgment of the truth. Jesus said, "Ye shall know the truth, and the truth shall make you free" (John 8:32). One of the unique features of Christianity is that it provides us with an ultimate freedom which is the basis of all freedoms. The Christian understands that he has been set free from spiritual tyranny and therefore he has a new relationship with society. He is not its victim, but, rather, he is a transforming agent of change within it.

Cosmic freedom from spiritual tyranny gives birth to freedom from social and political tyranny. No one had to order the early church to abolish slavery; it happened automatically because they realized that they were brothers and sisters equally free in the family of God. Throughout her history, the Church has always cried out against tyranny and injustice. She has demanded social and political freedom because she knew she was already free indeed.

Schaeffer argued that the Reformation brought the world the greatest freedoms it had ever known, yet without political chaos because society was culturally bound by a Christian consensus.[16] However, he warned, "When the memory of the Christian consensus which gave us freedom within biblical form is increasingly forgotten, a manipulating authoritarianism will tend to fill the vacuum. At this point the words 'right' and 'left' will make little difference. They are only two roads to the same end."[17]

Law and Order

Law and law enforcement go hand in hand. R. C. Sproul is correct when he observes that we cannot have law without law enforcement.[18] Ever since the Garden of Eden, the sword has been a symbol of restraint. Satan himself is described in Scripture as provoking the lawless spirit of disobedience.[19] Therefore, the sinful nature of man is in conflict with the laws of God. It is the source of individual and corporate evil in society and it must be restrained by law. The ultimate condition which results from lawlessness is chaos and anarchy. It is in this state that evil dominates all of society. Therefore, to hold human nature in check, God has ordained human government to protect, maintain, and sustain human life.

Saint Augustine called government "a necessary evil." Sproul explains, "By that he meant that government itself is made *necessary* by the fact of evil and even though governments may be oppressive and exploitive and corrupt, the worst government is still better than no government."[20] By contrast, Thomas Aquinas believed government was necessary to benefit the common good of mankind. As such it not only restrains evil, but promotes the common good of all.

The key biblical passage on the responsibility of the Christian to human government is found in Romans 13:1–7. Here the believer is told several things about government:

1. Political Authority Is Ordained by God. The Apostle Paul wrote: "The powers that be are ordained of God" (13:1). Therefore, all human authority is delegated and subject to the delegator,

66

who is God. The power of government is a God-given authority over our lives.

2. *Obedience Is a Religious Obligation.* The believer is commanded to obey civil authority and not to resist "the ordinance of God" (13:2). The Christian is to do all he can to obey the law and live peaceably with all men. However, his obedience is one of testimony, not blind obligation.

3. *Government Exists to Promote Justice.* Paul viewed the magistrate as a "minister of God" to whom honor was due. By this he acknowledged the responsibility of the government to protect its citizenry and promote their common good. Government is to be God's instrument of maintaining justice in society and restraining evil.

4. *Resistance Will Be Judged.* In this passage the believer is warned that resisting the authority of government is resisting the authority of God, who ordained it. The passage assumes that government to be just. This passage is not a command to submit to tyranny or injustice. At times, acts of civil disobedience are necessary when earthly authorities command us to violate the laws of God. Otherwise, every Nazi in Germany during World War II could blame his actions on Hitler's chain of command.[21]

5. *Hierarchy of Ethics.* Often the Christian is caught between moral obligations. He is told to obey the government which tells him to take another human life. He is then confronted with a hierarchy of ethical choices.[22] He must decide which values predominate over others. For example, if he is told to deny Christ, as were the early Christians, he must disobey the government in order to obey Christ's command not to deny Him before men (*see* Acts 5:29).

Separation of Church and State

The concept of the organizational separation of Church and State guaranteed by the Constitution has often been interpreted to mean the separation of God and State, as if the State ruled autonomously. The

State is not autonomous; it derives its authority from God by divine delegation. Therefore Sproul is right when he argues that it is "a legitimate vehicle" within which the people of God may serve.[23]

Serving one's fellow man as a Christian in government is a high and noble ideal. There we may bear witness to His truth, righteousness, and justice while representing our constituency well. This does not mean that we take the Church into the State, but that we take Christ into our statesmanship.

God rules in both spheres equally! He is sovereign over both the Church and the State. Nowhere does the Bible limit His authority to the spiritual domain; rather it acknowledges His supremacy over all creation. This is vital to the Christian understanding of Church and State. It is not us *against* them! The State is as subject to the sovereignty of God as is the Church. Therefore, Christ acknowledged the legitimate function of government when He said, "Render to Caesar the things that are Caesar's, and to God the things that are God's" (Mark 12:17). Since Caesar's authority is from God, he is under the sovereignty of God. That was the brilliance of Jesus' answer about the tribute coin.

"God and Caesar are not two separate realms," writes Paul Marshall in his classic study, *Thine Is the Kingdom*.[24] He goes on to observe that Paul's definition of human government in Romans 13 was a radical reevaluation of the accepted political order of the time. This view of government as the servant of God contradicted the emperor's claims to deity and supreme authority. The Bible denies this, clearly asserting that God is sovereign over all human authority. The State is not ultimate, but subordinate to God's authority.

To the Christian, Christ is the Lord of all life. Therefore, He is Lord ultimately of both kingdoms, earthly and heavenly. However, His Lordship is generally recognized only by His followers. Thus He said, "My kingdom is not of this world," and ordered His followers to put up the sword (*see* Matthew 26:52). Here true Christianity departs from crusading medieval Catholicism or militant Islam. The Gospel cannot be spread by the sword. Christ's Kingdom can only be advanced by its acceptance into the willing hearts of men and women.

This truth must be clearly understood by the New Right. We cannot force people into the Kingdom of Christ by political legislation. At the same time, we cannot sit idly by while anti-Christian forces attempt to eliminate God from American life and force upon us an unjust society. Government is force. Whoever controls it has the power to enforce its beliefs.

Here is where the tension exists in a democratic society. Competing forces are constantly battling for ideological control of the government. Thus it becomes very tempting for Christians to attempt to seize control in order to protect themselves or to promote their cause. While it is sometimes necessary to combat evil forces even in a democratic system, we must be careful to guarantee true freedom to all who may disagree with us. This is where those who hold to Dominion Theology take a different approach to transforming society.[25] They literally advocate that Christians take over the government in order to enforce biblical standards by law on the rest of society. Rather than seeking to influence the political process, they want nothing short of a total theocracy on their terms.[26]

Despite its problems, Dominion Theology has some very positive contributions to make to our understanding of the relationship of religion to society in general and politics in particular. Its adherents correctly emphasize that society is broader than politics and that it encompasses all social institutions, including church, state, and family. They argue for social justice in every area of life based upon biblical truth. In fact, Gary North warns the New Right that its conservatism is an "instinctive conservatism," and not one self-consciously grounded in the Bible. Unfortunately, he is right.

THE DOCTRINE OF DEMOCRACY?

If a Christian theocracy is not possible prior to the return of Christ, is democracy the next best option? Some in the New Right have actually implied that democracy is the God-ordained method of human government. Peter Marshall and David Manuel argue that America is a "chosen nation" and that its form of government was inspired by God.[27] In their best-seller, *The Light and the Glory,* they defend the proposition that America was founded as a Christian nation which must now return to its spiritual roots to enjoy His blessing.

A Chosen Nation

This theme is dominant in New Right thinking but is partly flawed. While it is true that God was sovereignly involved in founding this nation, He is no less sovereignly involved in the affairs of all nations. America has not been accorded "favored nation" status by God. What did benefit the United States was a broad dissemination of biblical knowledge which Francis Schaeffer called a "Christian Consensus."[28]

That consensus was crucial to the kind of nation the United States became. Schaeffer observed, "This does not mean that it was a golden age, nor that the founders were personally Christian, nor that those who were Christians were always consistent in their political thinking."[29] But, he went on to argue, their belief in a Creator to whom they were responsible and their commitment to biblical standards of morality made all the difference between the American Revolution and the French Revolution, or the later Russian Revolution.

Schaeffer added, "We must be careful, however, not to overstate the case and imply that the United States ever was a 'Christian nation' in a truly biblical sense of what it means to be a Christian, or that the United States could ever properly be called God's 'chosen nation.' "[30] What did happen in America, though, did not happen apart from God. No one can deny that this nation has thus far enjoyed unparalleled prosperity because of its adherence to biblical principles of freedom, justice, equality, integrity, honesty, and hard work.

If America has a manifest destiny, it is not clearly indicated in Scripture either prophetically or emphatically. That is not to say that she may not have a crucial role in history, for, indeed, she already has one. But what is unique about America is not the place itself but the people who live here, a good percentage of whom are professing Christians, as were many of her early settlers. For them, America was like a great island of freedom from the religious persecutions of Europe. But the same could be said of other nations to which believers fled as well.

A Theology of Democracy

Another attempt to define the relationship of the Bible to democracy is seen in the effort to establish a theological justification for democracy. In their book *Designed for Destiny,* Jerry Combee and Cline Hall identify what they call "doctrines of democracy."[31] These are: (1) equality of rights; (2) liberty for all; (3) limited government; (4) government by consent; (5) right of revolution. While there is certainly merit to these ideas, one would have a very difficult time proving their origins as imperatives in Scripture. Here we must be very careful not to read our preferences into Scripture, just as we would caution those who would advocate socialism and shared economic wealth on the basis of the Church's action in Acts 2:44–46 and 4:34, 35.

In contrast to democracy, the Old Testament advocated theocracy and tolerated monarchy. In the New Testament, the Church often suffered persecution under a totalitarian state. However, it could be argued that the principles of congregational church government articulated in the New Testament became the basis for the limited democracy of the Pilgrims and Puritans.[32] Nevertheless, their understanding and development of those principles has taken nearly three centuries to fully develop.

Biblical Principles

A third way to explain the relationship of the Bible to democracy is to identify the biblical principles that transcend political structures. Once these can be articulated, the question becomes, Which political system best incorporates these principles? The next question would be, How can that system be improved?

1. The Principle of Life.

And the Lord God formed man of the dust of the ground, and breathed into his nostrils the breath of life; and man became a living soul.

Genesis 2:7

Life is a gift from God. As Christians we must recognize that only God Almighty can create a life and that we have an obligation to honor and protect it. There are several propositions that emerge from this principle.

We must protect the existence of a human life. Since life is a gift from God and since we believe that life begins at conception, we believe that abortion is the murder of human life. Therefore we are committed to promote legislative and judicial relief from this genocide. Our concern for human life goes beyond abortion to euthanasia and infanticide. In their book *Whatever Happened to the Human Race?* Francis A. Schaeffer and Dr. C. Everett Koop ask, "Will a society which has assumed the right to kill infants in the womb— because they are unwanted, imperfect, or merely inconvenient— have difficulty in assuming the right to kill other human beings, especially older adults who are judged unwanted, deemed imperfect physically or mentally, or considered a possible social nuisance?"[33]

We must promote the dignity of human life. We believe that we were created in the image of God and as such we have great worth and merit. Consequently, we must do all that we can to enhance a person's dignity. We are opposed to any economic system that robs people of their worth and denies them their God-given creativity. We are concerned about the poor, the oppressed, and disenfranchised. We reject Marxism, socialism, and welfarism because we believe these systems lock people into oppression and hopelessness. While we must care for those who cannot help themselves, we must promote a system that restores dignity and worth to each individual. To rob people of this opportunity is to deny them part of God's creative intent.

We must promote the equality of human life.

> Red and yellow, black and white,
> All are precious in His sight.

These are more than the words of a simple Sunday School song. They are the expression of an important biblical truth. We are all equal before God. The New Testament clearly prohibits prejudicial and racist attitudes and actions (James 2). Such behavior is antithetical to Christianity. Fundamentalists should have been at the forefront of the civil rights movement but were not. We were wrong, and we do not intend now to sanction by our silence any system that denies people their equality before God and each other.

2. The Principle of Freedom

And the Lord God commanded the man, saying, Of every tree of the garden thou mayest freely eat: But of the tree of the knowledge of good and evil, thou shalt not eat of it: for in the day that thou eatest thereof thou shalt surely die.

Genesis 2:16, 17

Man was created *posse peccare et posse non peccare*. He was created with the freedom to choose. We are opposed to any system of government which seeks to oppress its constituents by eliminating their freedom of choice. We are committed to protecting the rights of human beings to choose their work and worship, their homes and cars, their vacations and recreation, their friends and colleagues, their groups and associations. We believe that we must be free to express our opinions and oppose others with whom we disagree. We believe that the most important choice is the freedom to worship God according to the dictates of our conscience. This religious freedom not only incorporates the freedom to worship, it includes the freedom to preach, to teach, to evangelize, and to exercise our responsibility to address the social and moral problems of society. We believe that this basic human right of freedom of choice transcends the dictates of the State and is rooted in our dignity as human beings created in the image of God.

3. The Principle of Sin.

And God saw that the wickedness of man was great in the earth, and that every imagination of the thoughts of his heart was only evil continually.

Genesis 6:5

Wherefore, as by one man sin entered into the world, and death by sin; and so death passed upon all men, for that all have sinned.

Romans 5:12

Fundamentalists and evangelicals believe in the depravity of human nature. In commenting on this doctrine, theologian Louis Berkof states, "The contagion of his sin at once spread through the entire man, leaving no part of his nature untouched, but violating every power and faculty of body and soul."[34] We believe that human beings are fallen creatures living in a fallen world. This theological doctrine has important bearing upon our understanding of biblical truth and its relevance to political and social involvement. First, in light of man's depravity, we believe that his ultimate hope is not in the reformation of society but in personal salvation through the Gospel of Jesus Christ. While social and political concern is legitimate, it can never replace the priority of calling fallen mankind to repentance and faith in Jesus Christ. In this sense, the Church must always remain the Church. Second, man's depravity has clear implications for political governance. Man's inherent quest for power and domination and his propensity for evil and destruction demand a system of governance that is predicated upon higher laws and limited government that respects the rights and freedoms of all.

For this reason we believe that the future of the American democratic society is predicated upon our allegiance and adherence to the principles of the Judeo-Christian ethic. Consequently, we are opposed to the current secularization of our society and believe that the exorcism of religion from the public square will inevitably result in the elimination of an objective higher moral standard. We will in essence lose the substantive foundation for the moral and ethical standards that guarantee the freedoms which we now enjoy.

Competing Moral Principles

While it is relatively easy to define and discuss these principles, it is infinitely more difficult to apply them to the complex problems of the twentieth century. In fact, these principles could conflict with each other amid attempts to solve the social evils of society.

74

The sin of apartheid in South Africa is such an example. First, apartheid is clearly a violation of the principle of life. It denies the dignity and equality of human beings under God. Christians ought to oppose it and bring whatever pressure necessary to eliminate it. However, when one calls for divestment and a further destabilization of the economy, the principle of freedom enters into the formula. South Africa is threatened by a Communist takeover. If this were to happen, the basic human right of freedom would be eliminated in favor of a godless, Marxist state. Consequently, there are Christians calling for divestment in the name of equality and Christians opposing divestment in the name of freedom. Both positions have merit.[35] The issue then becomes one of hierarchical moral principles. It becomes a matter of choosing the overriding moral principle for a complex moral problem.

The issue of nuclear armament is also an issue of competing moral principles. Our commitment to the protection of human life has important implications for nuclear arms. The threat of nuclear annihilation is a threat against the human race. As such, it is legitimate for Christians to oppose nuclear arms. However, our belief in the depravity of man forces us to take the threat of Soviet expansionism seriously. The expansionist arm of Communist domination has murdered 140-plus million people since 1917 and denied human rights to millions more. Consequently, opposing Communism is an act that protects basic human rights. In order to protect the freedom of the Western world, it is necessary to build an armament that will prevent the Soviets from further world domination. Therefore, the principles of life, freedom, and depravity are brought into conflict.

Democracy: Our Best Option

The ultimate question is which political structure is most suited to the expression and protection of those essential values. We suggest that the answer to that question is a democratic political system. This is not a theological answer predicated upon a series of biblical proof texts. Rather, it is a pragmatic answer rooted in historical evidence. Democratic governance guarantees the equality and dignity of human life. It also protects our basic human rights and guarantees our freedom of religion. It allows us to be what God has called us to be and to do what God has called us to do. Democratic governance is a governance of limited power and a system of checks and balances. It inhibits man's quest for absolute power and domination. While other political systems offer some of these benefits, democracy offers all of them. For Christians, it promises the best alternative for the expression of our values in a fallen world.

Chapter Five

Armageddon Theology: Preachers, Politics, and the End of the World

And he gathered them together into a place called in the Hebrew tongue Armageddon.

Revelation 16:16

 Evangelical Christians believe that we are living in the "end times" when the world will enter into a series of cataclysmic wars. Israel will suffer a terrible tribulation or persecution. By the time the wars end, perhaps as much as three-fourths of the earth's population will be destroyed. The Book of Ezekiel tells us that seven months will be spent burying the dead. These chilling events will precede the triumphant return of Christ to earth.

"Armageddon theology" is the popular term for an eschatological understanding of biblical prophecy about the end of the world. In secular America, these beliefs are little understood, but in the evangelical-fundamentalist world, they are heatedly promulgated and discussed on a regular basis. Some 50 million Americans who call themselves "born again" Christians agree with the basic tenets of that eschatology. No wonder that Hal Lindsey's book *The Late Great Planet Earth*, which expresses the evangelical understanding of the future, sold 15 million copies and was named by the *New York Times* as the best-seller of the 1970s.[1] These views on Bible prophecy have been proclaimed over the television airwaves by preachers such as Jerry Falwell, Pat Robertson, Jimmy Swaggart, Jim Bakker, and Jack Van Impe. And if evangelical involvement in the political process continues to grow, it is likely that Armageddon theology will also gain increasing exposure.

What Ronald Reagan thinks about it is not entirely clear. During the 1984 presidential debates, he was asked by Marvin Kalb, "Do you feel that we are now heading, perhaps, for some kind of nuclear Armageddon?" Nancy Reagan groaned, "Oh, no," but the president responded that he had spoken with theologians who felt that biblical prophecies were being fulfilled as never before. But "no one knows whether those prophecies mean that Armageddon is a thousand years away or the day after tomorrow. So I have never seriously warned and said we must plan according to Armageddon."[2] If Reagan's degree of agreement with the theologians is uncertain, his affirmation of the inevitability of such a conflict was to many a shocking admission.

For a variety of reasons, the notion of Armageddon theology is deeply troubling to many Christians, Jews, and secularists. Their concern surfaced during the 1984 campaign when 100 religious leaders, including William Sloane Coffin and Bishop Thomas Gumbleton, held a press conference to announce that it was "profoundly disturbing" that political leaders "might identify with extremists who believe that nuclear war is inevitable and imminent." After all, this could easily lead one to conclude "that reconciliation with America's adversaries is ultimately futile." The liberal Christic Institute went further, charging that evangelicals were using prophecy "to justify nuclear war as a divine instrument to punish the wicked and complete God's plan for history."[3]

Apparently many believe that because evangelicals look forward to the Second Coming of Christ, they will try to hasten that event. They are often accused of trying to foment a crisis in the Middle East that could lead to a Soviet war with Israel, or to provoke a showdown between the United States and the Soviet Union. Some people who understand the belief that born again Christians will be "raptured" or taken out of the world before the final Tribulation charge that believers are indifferent to peace-making efforts, since they do not think they will suffer the consequences of the war of Armageddon.[4]

Christians who believe that the forces of God will triumph ultimately over the forces of evil sometimes ask why evangelicals would hesitate to get into a war they are theologically assured of winning. Finally, there is a general concern about the widespread conversion of non-Christians, especially Jews, which is said to attend the end times. These arguments, however, are based on a profound misunderstanding of the Bible and what evangelicals actually believe. In order to understand this issue, it is important to understand something of the history of millennial prophecy—a very old idea which has suffered many setbacks.

VIEW OF ESCHATOLOGY

Both the Old and New Testaments speak about the end of the world. The prophet Joel called it the "day of the Lord." He foresaw a day of thick darkness, gloominess, clouds, and a devouring fire (*see* Joel 2:1–3). The prophet Isaiah called it the "time of vengeance of our God" (*see* Isaiah 34:2–9). The Apostle Peter predicted, ". . . The elements shall melt with fervent heat, the earth also and the works that are therein shall be burned up" (2 Peter 3:10). The Apostle Paul warned that ". . . the Lord Jesus shall be revealed from heaven with his mighty angels, in flaming fire taking vengeance on them that know not God . . ." (2 Thessalonians 1:7, 8). The Book of Revelation says the air will be darkened, water polluted, and great rivers dried up. Earthquakes will shake the planet, and Babylon will be devoured by fire. Concurrent with these visions of destruction are prophecies of the coming millennial (thousand year) reign of Jesus Christ.

For centuries, Christians and others have tried to attach dates to these prophecies, with a spectacular lack of success. As early as the second century A.D., Montanus predicted that Christ would soon return to set up His Kingdom in Phrygia in Asia Minor. Since then, other candidates for the New Jerusalem have included Rome, Constantinople, London, Muenster, and Chicago. The Mormons think it will be Salt Lake City, although a vocal group of Mormon dissidents insists it will be Independence, Missouri.[5]

One Puritan writer said that Christ would return in 1666.[6] When that didn't happen, another extended the deadline to 1690.[7] In the aftermath of the Reformation, a group of Christians took over Muenster in Germany; their parliament actually held debates on whether a man on horseback seen riding through the area was Christ returned to earth.[8] When French troops temporarily drove the Pope from Rome in 1798, one premillennialist predicted that the Battle of Armageddon had already begun—the Catholics were identified as the forces of antichrist.[9]

In the early nineteenth century, a Baptist preacher named William Miller predicted that Christ would return in 1844; Miller arrived at that date by converting the 2,300 days of the Book of Daniel (8:14) into years. When 1844 passed, Miller gave up on the scheme, but many of his followers did not—they formed what later became known as the Seventh Day Adventists.[10] At the end of the nine-teenth century, Charles Russell forecast that Christ would return visibly in 1916. He didn't, so his followers—who called themselves the Jehovah's Witnesses—claimed Christ came secretly and ushered in the Kingdom Age. Thus, Jehovah's Witnesses meet in "kingdom halls."[11]

Our own century has seen its share of date-setting and millennial prediction. Herbert Armstrong declared that the end of the world would come in January 1972, and some of his followers in the Worldwide Church of God promptly sold their possessions and took to the hills.[12] Television preacher Jack Van Impe announced that the Communists would invade the United States in 1976. The symbol 666 from the Book of Revelation has been identified with Hitler, Mussolini, Franklin Roosevelt, the National Council of Churches, Henry Kissinger, and Anwar Sadat, to name a few. Even Ronald Wilson Reagan, whose three names all have six letters, has been identified as the antichrist. In the face of all this, it may seem hard to take biblical prophecy seriously at all. But evangelicals do.

In understanding the evangelical view of biblical prophecy, it is crucial to define three very different systems of eschatology. Each views the end times very differently, and consequently the political implications are quite different.

The *postmillennial* school believes that Christ will return after the

Millennium to announce that His Kingdom on earth has been realized. Postmillennialists believe that during the Millennium, the Church should conquer unbelief and convert the vast majority of people to Christianity, and that society should be run according to biblical law. In this way, they seek to usher in the Second Coming of Christ. Postmillennial advocates have included Catholics, Puritans, and some modern day fundamentalists and charismatics. They emphasize "Dominion Theology" and argue that Christians are to take dominion over the earth in order to actualize the Kingdom of God on earth.[13]

Amillennial theology sees no literal Millennium on earth. It tends to view events described in the Book of Revelation as referring to the Church Age—the time when Christianity exerts a powerful influence on people and overcomes the forces of evil. References to the "thousand years" are interpreted as symbolic. Amillennialists believe that Christ will return when He returns, and immediately conduct the Last Judgment. Two elements of amillennialism are preeminent in its eschatology. First, all of God's promises to Israel are viewed as being fulfilled in the New Testament Church. Thus, amillennialists see no specific future for national Israel. Instead, they view the Church as "spiritual" Israel. Secondly, amillennialists have traditionally argued for an extensive involvement of the Church in cultural, social, and political affairs. They view the present era as the ultimate conflict between the forces of good and evil.[14]

Finally there is *premillennialism,* which holds that Christ will return before the Millennium and then reign on the earth for a thousand years. Most premillennialists do not believe Christians will be present on earth during the last days to witness the wars, tribulation, and the Christian conversion of the state of Israel. Because premillennialists do not believe that society must be prepared for a thousand years for Christ's Second Coming, they reject the idea of imposing biblical law on unbelievers. Premillennialists are by far the dominant strain in evangelical eschatology.[15] Traditionally premillennialists have avoided any involvement in American political and social issues. Those who also believe in a pretribulational Rapture generally have been content to wait for Christ to come and remove the Church from this evil society.

We should further note that premillennialists are themselves subdivided into three camps:

1. *Pre-Tribulationalists* believe that Christ will return in the air to rapture the Church before the Tribulation begins on earth. After seven years of tribulation, Christ will return with His Church to defeat the forces of antichrist and establish the Kingdom of God on earth.[16]

2. *Mid-Tribulationalists* believe that the Church will go through the first three and one-half years of the Tribulation period and be raptured at the mid-point of the seven years of total tribulation. Those advocating this view emphasize the prophetic use of the phrase "time, times, and a half a time" to refer to three and one-half years.[17]

3. *Post-Tribulationalists* believe the Church will go through the entire seven-year Tribulation period on earth at the end of the present Church Age. Thus, these interpreters view the suffering "saints" in the prophecies of Revelation as Christians, not converted Jews.[18]

With such diverse evangelical opinion, it is folly to label any one view as *the* evangelical eschatology. Unfortunately, however, this is often done by the media because of the popularization of the pre-tribulational and premillennial views of the most popular television preachers. Of all the TV pastors, only James Kennedy and Robert Schuller shy away from this position, preferring the amillennial perspective.[19] This also explains why Kennedy and Schuller do not share the other televangelists' enthusiasm for the modern state of Israel, since they believe that God's promises to Israel were allegorically fulfilled in the New Israel, that is, the Christian Church.

POSTMILLENNIAL VISIONS OF A NEW THEOCRACY

Apocalyptic visions of the end of the world are nothing new. They have played an important role throughout Church history and have been especially predominant in the history of the Protestant movement.

As early as the Middle Ages, John Wycliffe (1329–1384) suggested that the Catholic Pope was the antichrist and that Protestants were engaged in an apocalyptic war with the corrupted papacy.[20] This idea greatly influenced Calvin and Martin Luther. Many Protestant reformers identified the years A.D. 500 to A.D. 1500 as the Millennium of the "legitimate papacy," after which they felt it was corrupted by Satan. These reformers believed the Reformation represented an attempt by Protestants to expel the satanic evil before the final conflict of Armageddon.[21]

The early reformers viewed the years from A.D. 500 to A.D. 1500 as the thousand years when Satan was bound on earth (*see* Revelation 20:1–7). During this time the spread of the Gospel flourished in Europe. Using this scheme, they further surmised that Satan was now loosed to deceive the nations. They identified him with the papacy, which they now viewed as wicked and corrupt.

The reformers believed that they were engaged in the final, apocalyptic struggle with Satan and the forces of antichrist. For example, the Puritans were postmillennialists who believed they were living in the last part of the thousand years after which Christ would come. The Cromwellian revolution was, to them, the "Battle of God and Magog"; in other words, the final conflict. Puritans called for the complete expulsion of the forces of antichrist embodied in the monarch, Charles I. The notable Puritan divine, John Owen, told Parliament that Charles's execution was a "fulfillment of prophecy."[22]

But Charles died and Christ did not return. Soon Puritan eschatology began to shift from postmillennialism toward premillennialism. No longer was the Church seen as a mechanism for bringing about Christ's Second Coming. Hope was placed, instead, in waiting for Christ, who would fulfill what the Church had failed to accomplish.[23]

The New World saw a revival of postmillennialism. Puritans in America identified their country with the New Jerusalem. God would establish His Kingdom on earth on the shores of the New World, they said. During the Great Awakening of the 1740s, Jonathan Edwards enthusiastically predicted that the Millennium was coming to an end and that Christ would return shortly. The millennial enthusiasm of the Great Awakening played an important role in the American Revolution.[24]

Postmillennialism remained a dominant force in American Protestantism throughout the eighteenth and nineteenth centuries. But postmillennialist notions of a world bringing itself more into line with God to prepare for His return were shattered by twentieth-century catastrophes, such as the Nazi holocaust and Stalin's genocide. Far from moving toward greater conversion and a closer following of biblical law, the world seemed to be moving away from it. Today postmillennialism is mainly a legacy. Jerry Falwell has said that it is harder to find a postmillennialist now than a Wendell Willkie button.

One exception to this trend is Rousas J. Rushdoony and his Chalcedon group. Rushdoony is a highly regarded biblical scholar who is advocating the reconstruction of American society based upon biblical law. An early supporter of the Moral Majority, Rushdoony not only advocates the necessity of Christian influence in society, but the total conquest of society by Christians.[25]

Rushdoony wants to replace secular law with biblical law. He has outlined his vision in *Institutes of Biblical Law,* regarded as his masterwork. In it, he calls for "the saints of the world," that is, Christians, "to prepare to take over the world's government and its courts." Rushdoony distrusts democracy—in fact, he maintains that "the choice, ultimately, is the basic one between democracy and traditional Christian theology"—but he believes that fundamentalists must use the democratic process to come to power, and then end democracy. Some of Rushdoony's followers, in order to prepare the world for Christ's Second Coming, have called for laws mandating the death penalty for homosexuals and drunkards.[26]

Rushdoony's views may be frightening to many secularists and members of the Jewish, Moslem, and Buddhist faiths, but the views are also at odds with premillennialist and amillennialist Christian thought. Unfortunately, *Newsweek* has labeled Rushdoony's Chalcedon Foundation as the think tank of the Religious Right.[27] Indeed, confusion abounds. Rushdoony and his compatriots are regular guests on religious television and radio shows and have won a number of adherents among the charismatics, despite their ardent

Calvinism. Their books are being published by standard evangelical publishers and their works have received approving comments by Jerry Falwell and the late Francis Schaeffer.[28]

The basic tenets of Rushdoony's Reconstructionism are:

1. *Presuppositional apologetics*. This is the belief that the Bible is the only legitimate source of Christian truth and that intellectual appeals to reason are useless apart from the convicting power of the Holy Spirit.[29]
2. *Theonomy*. Following their Puritan forefathers, theonomists argue for the government of society by the rule of biblical law. Some Reconstructionists have gone as far as advocating the eventual abolition of democracy and the imposition of Old Testament animal sacrifices.[30]
3. *Postmillennialism*. As already discussed, this view of eschatology is predominant in their system. They do not view the world as a sinking ship, but rather as one that needs to be commandeered and given direction.

The ultimate application of Rushdoony's Reconstructionism would eliminate pluralism in American society in the name of denying legitimacy to non-Christian beliefs. Ironically, many of those who claim to hold democracy so dear have found a temporary ally in one who is inherently opposed to democracy and pluralism.

AMILLENNIALISM AND THE DEMOCRATIC PROCESS

The history of amillennialism as a precise eschatological view is difficult to trace. It is generally accepted that Augustine of Hippo first articulated this view by arguing that the Millennium was to be interpreted allegorically as referring to the Church in which Christ reigned in His saints.[31] While this view was challenged in the medieval church by men like Joachim of Fiore, it remained the dominant view until the time of the Protestant Reformation. Both Luther and Calvin were suspicious of millennial speculation, but their followers were not.[32]

Amillennialism has several unique features. Since it views the Church as the Kingdom of Christ on earth, its adherents are not looking for the coming of the Kingdom as are premillennialists, and they are not trying to bring in the Kingdom as are postmillennialists. Rather they believe that the Kingdom is already present in the Church on earth. Therefore, amillennialists are very committed to expressing the character of Christ to the secular world by influencing the political process.[33]

In American politics, amillennialists have generally been very supportive of democratic pluralism. They believe that Christians are to be the spiritual "salt of the earth" within that process. As such they see their role as that of attracting nonbelievers to the truth by an exemplary life-style. Thus, the believer best influences society by being a true Christian in all his dealings with society.

Amillennialism is the predominant eschatology of today's Presbyterians, Lutherans, and Methodists. It is also held by religious groups as divergent as Catholics and Baptists. In general, amillennialists view the present church age as the time when Christ is ruling His Kingdom on earth in the lives of true believers.

The present era, they believe, will end with the return of Christ to judge the world, probably through a literal Armageddon, and then to usher in eternity. According to this eschatological scheme, believers go right from the present into a heavenly eternity. Amillennialism does not look forward to a millennial reign of Christ on earth in the future. Therefore, its adherents do not look for a Jewish kingdom in which Christ will literally rule the earth from the throne of David in Jerusalem. Thus, the amillennialists' attention is on the Church's role *in* society.

DISPENSATIONAL PREMILLENNIALISM AND THE RAPTURE

The overwhelming majority of evangelicals and fundamentalists would describe themselves as premillennialists. Actually, they would say they are premillennial dispensationalists. Dispensationalism refers to an eschatological perspective that sees history as a series of "dispensations," or ages, with Christ's return coming at the end. The major fundamentalist seminaries and many televangelists hold this position. Their views have often been criticized as relying on the Rapture as the "Great Escape."

Premillennial dispensationalism was propagated in the nineteenth century by the Plymouth Brethren movement in England. John Nelson Darby (1800–1882) was its most prominent spokesman. It spread to the United States, where the Bible Conference movement brought it into hundreds of thousands of homes.[34] The *Scofield Reference Bible* of the Reverend C. I. Scofield contained extensive notes about dispensationalism.[35] Premillennial dispensationalists tend to identify the final dispensation—the Age of Apostasy—with the rise of theological liberalism in the twentieth century.

Premillennialists believe that the end times will be harbingered by the Rapture, which refers to the literal absorption of Christians into heaven. By Christians, they do not mean all professing Christians; rather, those who have accepted Jesus Christ as their personal Savior. The Rapture is suggested by several biblical passages, notably Saint Paul's First Letter to the Thessalonians, in which he says, "For the Lord himself shall descend from heaven with a shout, with the voice of the archangel, and with the trump of God: and the dead in Christ shall rise first: Then we which are alive and remain shall be caught up together with them in the clouds, to meet the Lord in the air: and so shall we ever be with the Lord" (1 Thessalonians 4:16, 17).

Popular evangelical pastor and author Tim LaHaye outlines what might ensue after Rapture: "The Rapture will be an event of such startling proportions that the entire world will be conscious of our leaving. There will be airplane, bus and train wrecks throughout the world. Who can imagine the chaos on the freeways when automobile drivers are snatched out of their cars? One cannot help surmise that many strangers will be in churches the first Sunday after the Rapture. Liberal churches, where heretics in clerical garb have not preached the Word of God, may be filled to capacity with wondering and frantic church members."[36]

Most evangelicals think that the Tribulation will follow the Rapture. The main reason is that Christian churches are never referred to in the Bible after its account of the Rapture. The Bible says that Christians as a force for good will simply be removed from the world, and evil will run rampant. This will correspond with the rise of a force of evil such as the world has never seen before—the antichrist. In a pamphlet on Armageddon theology, Jimmy Swaggart notes that all the world's dictators— Genghis Khan, Attila the Hun, Hitler, Stalin—acted in the spirit of the antichrist but could not rival his supreme evil. Evangelicals believe that the antichrist will make the tyrants of the past seem benign by comparison—and the main target of his fury will be Israel.[37]

Dispensationalists believe that the Tribulation will largely consist of the antichrist persecuting the Jews and the nation of Israel. This, they believe, will be "the time of Jacob's trouble" referred to in Scripture.[38] Most fundamentalists also believe that the Soviet Union will form an alliance with various Arab countries and eventually invade Israel. Pat Robertson told *U.S. News and World Report,* "I have felt that one day the Soviet Union or its satellites will invade Israel."[39]

Dispensationalist theologian Dwight Pentecost of Dallas Theological Seminary has said that "God's purpose for Israel in this Tribulation is to bring about the conversion of a multitude of Jews, who will enter into the blessings of the Kingdom and experience the fulfillment of all Israel's covenants."[40] He views the Tribulation as ending with the conversion of Israel and the total defeat of the forces of the Soviet Union and the antichrist. Following this will be a literal thousand-year reign of Christ on earth preceding the Last Judgment.

Ever since the early part of this century, premillennial evangelicals have tended to view the end of the world as imminent, and consequently they have withdrawn themselves from the institutions of society, regarding political and social reform as futile. They have focused their efforts on evangelistic attempts to win converts to Christ. Some of the more extreme fundamentalists have virtually given up on the world. Their eschatology has made them complacent about such issues as nuclear proliferation, peace in the Middle East, or any attempts to resolve international conflict with the Soviet Union. Theirs is a dispensationalist fatalism of the worst sort.

ESCHATOLOGICAL REALISM

Apocalyptic eschatological speculation is certainly a dangerous business because it has dangerous implications when applied to political and social structures. One had better be certain he is right before proceeding too far with his vision for the end.

Despite the problems, there is much that is valuable in the eschatological enterprise. Despite their differences, every school of eschatological thought points to the eventual triumph of Christ over the forces of evil. The tough questions are *when* and *how?*

One of the apparently more successful eschatological speculators was the amazing Harry Rimmer.[41] His books, *The Shadow of Coming Events* and *The Coming War and the Rise of Russia,* were written in the 1940s during World War II. Taking Ezekiel's prophecies as his guide, Rimmer forecast early during the war that the Axis powers would lose, that Italy would lose her colonial holdings in North Africa, including Libya and Ethiopia, and that Russia would emerge from the war as the major enemy of Israel and the West. He said this at a time when the Soviet Union was an ally to the United States and Roosevelt was posing amicably with Stalin. Naturally, Rimmer's standing in the evangelical community rose tremendously after his interpretation proved correct.

Unlike the foretellers of the medieval age, evangelicals today do not juggle with biblical numbers to come up with dates. Rather, they follow a literal understanding of Scripture which is very consistent with their general biblical hermeneutic. Perhaps the keystone prophecy which confirms their conviction that these are the end times is the return of the Jews to their ancestral homeland. This is unequivocally forecast in the Bible.[42]

"When Israel was founded in 1948," writes Hal Lindsey in *The Late Great Planet Earth,* "the prophetic countdown began."[43] Many Christians believe that Israel's capture of Old Jerusalem in 1967 is also very significant, because it makes possible the rebuilding of the Holy Temple in Jerusalem. They believe that this is a key biblical sign preceding the Second Coming. Fundamentalists interpret Christ's forecast about the end times—"This generation shall not pass, till all these things be fulfilled" (Matthew 24:34)—as referring to the generation that comes after the founding of Israel; in other words, our generation.[44]

Of course, it is theoretically possible that the Jews will once again be driven from Israel and return at some point in the future to participate in the Apocalypse. But common sense dictates that this is very unlikely. Both Jews and Gentiles, both Christians and secularists, agree and recognize that the formation of the state of Israel is an event of the greatest importance. After some two thousand years of exclusion, the Jews repossess their God-given home. Many believe this to be a precursor for the end of the age.

Recently, there has been a considerable segment of the secular community who agree that we are approaching the end of the world. Several Nobel laureates and reputable scientists tell us that the earth's clock may be running low. We hear so much about the possibility of nuclear holocaust and extinction—the very gloomy and apocalyptic vision of Jonathan Schell's *The Fate of the Earth,* for example. When evangelicals predicted the end of the world in earlier centuries, people laughed at them because the destruction of the entire planet was simply inconceivable. But today it is well within the realm of possibility. In fact, some secularists seem far more worried about it than fundamentalists are. They are not, however, accused of trying to hasten the end; indeed, they are often credited with the moral vision that is needed to forestall such an outcome.

We also recognize that Scripture tells us that no one knows when the end will come. Jesus Himself said, "But of that day and hour knoweth no man, no, not the angels of heaven, but my Father only" (Matthew 24:36). Saint Paul writes of the end, "But of the times and the seasons, brethren, ye have no need that I write unto you. For yourselves know perfectly that the day of the Lord so cometh as a thief in the night" (1 Thessalonians 5:1, 2).[45] It is foolish to act according to timetables when God advises against it. Fortunately, having learned from the errors of the past, fewer and fewer evangelical pastors are doing this.

Just as there are many Bible passages that describe the end times, there are scores of passages that outline Christian responsibilities in this world. We must take both sets of passages seriously. The Bible says that we should be ready for the Second Coming and that we should be good citizens—the salt of the earth. We do not view those missions as contradictory or mutually exclusive. We must work to better the world because the Bible tells us to, and we must await

Christ's return because the Scripture commands us to do so. In Luke 19:13, Jesus told His disciples to "occupy till I come." He meant that we are to be busy about His work, not merely occupying a seat. The idea of this word in the original Greek means to conquer as an occupying army.[46]

"The Bible says that as much as is possible in you, live in peace with all men," Pat Robertson told *Time* magazine in a recent interview.[47] He is justified by Matthew's Gospel, which says "Blessed are the peacemakers." The thirteenth chapter of Romans is full of instructions to Christians about their responsibility to civil government. We know that we must render unto Caesar as well as unto God.

This is why evangelicals and fundamentalists are investing so heavily in the future. All the major conservative Christian groups are building churches and schools and setting up missionary outposts abroad. Most have plans that already go into the twenty-first century. We would not make these plans if we were sure the world would soon be destroyed.

On the contrary, most evangelical preachers are in the arena of politics today to improve secular society, not abandon it. They are working hard to stop abortion, to improve the public schools, and to eliminate pornography. Most of us believe that it is our mandate from God to help make the world a better place to live and to use Christianity as a force for good in this world. We are advocating positive change. We believe life is a gift from God and that it is our duty to protect it. Our involvement clearly indicates that we are not among those whose apocalyptic views are a pretext for this-worldly despair.

While Christians may disagree among themselves on their views of eschatology and on the proper political response based upon them, one thing is clear: We are getting closer to the end with every day that passes. Our belief in Armageddon does not mean that we want to hasten its coming.

A TIME TO REPENT

A lot of the talk about speeding up the Apocalypse would be stopped if more people understood that prophecy cannot be altered.

There are some conditional prophecies; in the Old Testament, for example, when people repented for their sins, God would abstain from sending down a divine punishment. But the prophecies about the end times are unconditional. It is arrogant and sinful to think that we can change them. Pat Robertson has said that Armageddon is "an act of God Almighty that has nothing to do with human abilities whatsoever. I have no intention of helping God along in this respect."[48]

The only appropriate response to these prophecies, we believe, is to repent for our sins and try to bring as many people as possible to Christ. Our political concerns can never diminish the ultimate priority of evangelism. Jesus told His disciples, "Go ye into all the world, and preach the gospel to every creature" (Mark 16:15). He further added, ". . . that repentance and remission of sins should be preached in his name among all nations . . ." (Luke 24:47).

The Great Commission of our Lord to "make disciples of all nations" (*see* Matthew 28:19) does not promote coerced conversion. Rather, it clearly implies a voluntary acceptance of Christ as Savior and Lord. Even in these last days as we await His return, our biblical obligation is not to bring all men to Christ, but to bring Christ to all men.

Chapter Six

The Race for the Twenty-first Century

This know also, that in the last days perilous times shall come.

2 Timothy 3:1

God never promised that things would get easier as we neared the end of the age. In fact, premillennarians believe that things will get worse before they get better. This does not mean, however, that they will necessarily get worse during our lifetime or that the end must come any time soon. While we anticipate the return of Christ at any moment, we must also recognize that we cannot avoid our citizenship responsibilities in the meantime.

The twentieth century has brought the most incredible changes imaginable to the human race. Automobiles, airplanes, radios, televisions, and computers have thrust us into an environment our forefathers never could have envisioned. Whether we like it or not, each one of us is affected by modern technology daily and that technology is shaping our lives. It is no wonder that historian Paul Johnson called these days *Modern Times*.[1]

Yet with the advancement of modernity has come a restless uneasiness about the traditional values that are slipping away from our society. At times consciously and at other times unconsciously, we seem to be discarding the very ideas which built this great society. It would even seem that we have exchanged our souls for a technological "mess of pottage."

As the twentieth century sped along, secularism began to replace the Judeo-Christian values of our society. God was gradually but systematically removed from any place of prominence in our intellectual lives. Scientism emerged, turning pure science into a "religion" which taught that natural laws, not spiritual principles, guided the universe.[2]

The entrenchment of the theory of evolution made God unnecessary in our culture. Many people actually felt betrayed, because their belief in God had enabled them to believe in their own worth and dignity as well. Life had meaning and purpose as people lived to bring glory to God. But now those ideas have been swept away by the intellectual broom of secularism. Man now sees himself as little more than a glorified animal whose highest instincts are to satisfy his own selfish desires.

THE CULT OF SELFISM

Ours has become an age of self-gratification. The selfish pursuit of money, power, and fame have propelled us along a road headed toward disaster. Our whole society seems caught up in this rush for prosperity. Issues of character and personal integrity have been pushed aside in the desire for self-gratification.

Ours has been called an age of narcissism. There is now even a popular magazine called *Self*. The thrust of this self-appeasing approach to life is further advanced by the increased materialism of our society. The television game shows play on this concept, appealing to the viewer with an array of easily acquired material goods.

The average American knows little or nothing of real poverty by Third World standards. Americans think a financial disaster is losing the hubcap off your Lincoln or having one of your three television sets break down! We are so blessed with prosperity that we cannot imagine how the rest of the world lives, let alone really care.

As we near the end of the twentieth century, we are entering into an era of a global economy. We are no longer a loose collection of isolated communities, nor are we any longer an isolated nation. We are part of the global community. Telephones, satellites, and computers can transfer information all over the world in a matter of seconds. Airplanes can take us anywhere we want to go in a few hours. Every new advancement of technology brings us closer to the rest of the world.

THE REIGN OF RELATIVISM

One of the philosophical concepts that dominates the thinking of people today is the concept of relativism.[3] It is the opposite of absolutism and teaches that all truth is relative to its context. There are no absolutes according to this belief. Absolute truth is an impossibility in a world of relative contingencies. Something is "true" only because a majority of people accept it as truth. In reality, this theory views all issues as subject to human interpretation at a given point in time. In other words, what is considered to be true in one culture may not be true in another.

Relativism dethrones all absolutes, including divine law. It not only rejects the teachings of Scripture as binding upon human behavior, but it even rejects the very concept of "scripture." According to relativism, a writing is considered "scripture" only because a society deems it so. The writing is not viewed as inherently divine in nature. Therefore, relativism views the Bible on the same level as the Koran, or the Tripitakas of Buddha, or the Hindu Vedas. In some cases, modern critics have even suggested that other writings are superior to the Bible.

The influence of relativism has affected nearly every area of modern thinking. Once one accepts the basic premise of relativism, he no longer views truth as an absolute proposition.[4] The great danger of this concept is that it leads to a naive acceptance of the consequences of secularism. Under this system of thought, even the concepts of good and evil are viewed as culturally conditioned, and therefore relative to the perspective of that culture. Thus, even murder is not considered inherently wrong. It is only wrong because society deems it wrong.

HAVE WE LOST OUR MINDS?

One of the most powerful books to appear in this decade is Allan Bloom's *The Closing of the American Mind.*[5] Written by the professor of social thought at the University of Chicago, this blockbuster best-seller explores the intellectual vacuum of our time. Bloom argues that today's students are unlike any generation that has preceded them. They are headed, in his opinion, to intellectual oblivion because of the relativism that has permeated our culture.

Bloom calls his volume "a meditation on the state of our souls."[6] Though the book is not written from a Christian standpoint, it raises many issues which Christians have been raising for years. He argues that students have been so conditioned by our educational system to believe that all truth is relative that they are devoid of absolutes on which to build their lives. As a result, he explains, our culture has drifted with the winds of self-gratification.[7]

"Today's students are no longer interested in noble causes," Bloom bemoans. He explains that they are not committed to noble ideas and therefore are incapable of developing noble goals. Since relativity prevails, it robs ideology of nobility and the student is left with an overload of information which cannot change his life. "There is an indifference to such things," Bloom explains, "for relativism has extinguished the real motive of education."[8]

Bloom astutely observes that television, videos, and movies have replaced books in the lives of today's students, many of whom own more videocassettes than they do textbooks. Books have only become a means to an end, the professor explains. No longer do students cherish books like good friends. Books are to be used and then discarded, not cherished and preserved.[9] He charges that if the dean threatened to take away the students' books, they would probably cheer, but if he threatened to take away television sets or rock music cassettes, they would revolt!

Bloom is especially concerned about the self-centeredness of today's students. "Students these days are, in general, nice," he says. But, he adds, "They are not particularly moral or noble." The author observes that they are the product of good times when "neither tyranny nor want has hardened them or made demands on them.'' As a result, he warns that young people today have abandoned themselves to the pursuit of the ''good life.''[10]

A SOCIETY WITHOUT LEADERS

Unfortunately, the current quest of most students is for money, sex, power, and pleasure. It should not surprise us that these are problems for Christians as well, because they are the dead-end options of a society stuck on itself.

Bloom writes, ''Country, religion, family, ideas of civilization, all the sentimental and historical forces that stood between cosmic infinity and the individual, providing some notion of a place within the whole, have been rationalized away and have lost their compelling force.''[11] He also adds that we are now experiencing what de Tocqueville, the French admirer of American democracy, warned would ultimately lead to the ''disappearance of citizens and statesmen.'' In other words, everybody is caught up in ''making it'' for himself and really isn't interested in the common good of others.

The rise of individualism, coupled with the decline of the traditional family, has left us with a generation that has a tough time making commitments. This tendency shows up in almost every area of life, from choosing a career, to holding a job, to getting married. Reluctance to commit oneself to a belief or ideal is the inevitable result of relativism in our culture. We have a situation akin to the days of the biblical judges, when ''every man did that which was right in his own eyes.''

GOING FIRST CLASS ON THE TITANIC

Another educator, Arthur Levine, has described the current student mentality as that of going first class on the Titanic.[12] What he means is that students not only have become self-centered, but they have also given up any real hope of solving the world's problems. They view society as a sinking ship that will never reach its ultimate destination. They view themselves as stuck on a hopeless voyage. Since they can't get off, they simply clamor for the first-class seats on the top deck so that they can enjoy the ride until disaster strikes.

In other words, if they are going to be stuck on the *Titanic*, they intend to make the best of it until it is over.

Whether we like it or not, most of us are products of our times. As Christians, we must literally fight against the undercurrent of secularism and relativism which is sweeping away our Judeo-Christian foundation. Today's Christian students must be willing to swim upstream against the intellectual tide if they hope to make any real difference in our society. Claiming to be a Christian really isn't enough anymore; we must be willing to show it by our lives.

The choices we make regarding the investment of our lives will reflect whether we are committed to ourselves or others. In a time when most people are choosing to live for themselves, we must be willing to demonstrate the reality of Christ by living for Him and investing ourselves in others. This is the real key to finding meaning and purpose in one's life.

THE APPEASEMENT OF EVIL

The greatest danger of relativism is that it leads to the eventual appeasement of evil. If all truth is relative, then no belief is worth dying for. If I have part of the truth and you have part of the truth, then neither of us has the whole truth. Once we accept this concept, we have no basis upon which to judge actions as morally right or wrong. Thus it should not surprise us that secular society is willing to tolerate abortion, euthanasia, and even infanticide. The unborn, the elderly, the retarded, and the handicapped all become expendable by such logic.[13]

Surgeon General C. Everett Koop calls this indifference to the sanctity of life the "slide to Auschwitz."[14] Once philosophers, theologians, and medical personnel adopt such a view, a growing loss of human dignity will automatically occur. This is the same intellectual journey that led to the acceptance of Hitler's Nazi atrocities. A change in the moral climate toward human life is all that is necessary for the systematic elimination of undesirable life forms to become the norm.

Australian ethicist Peter Singer recently said, "We can no longer base our ethics on the idea that human beings are a special form of creation, made in the image of God, singled out from all other animals, and alone possessing an immortal soul."[15] In commenting on Singer's statement, Cal Thomas observes that removing the protective layer of man's uniqueness leaves him as vulnerable as a dog or a pig in the discussion about who or what ought to live—an assertion that Singer himself makes![16]

In commenting on the seriousness of abortion, Stuart Briscoe says, "Destruction of that made in the image of God challenges the divine intention. If God makes man for eternity and gives him the ability to function in relationship to Him, anyone who kills that man destroys what God had in mind. The destroyer shakes his fist in the face of God."[17]

A HUMANISTIC VIEW OF GOVERNMENT

Humanism is that form of secularism that views man, not God, as the central reality of life. Gloria Steinem, editor of *MS.* magazine and recipient of the 1978 American Humanist Association Pioneer Award, said, "By the year 2000 we will, I hope, raise our children to believe in human potential, not God."[18] Humanists, in general, believe that man must solve his own problems apart from any divine guidance. Thus secular humanism and relativism are the philosophic bases of modern liberalism.

Tim LaHaye has defined secular humanism as "a Godless, man-centered philosophy of life that rejects moral absolutes and traditional values."[19] He argues that secular humanists "have relentlessly sought to secularize" our nation by influencing legislative and judicial governmental control in every area of our society, including the Church and the family.

R. C. Sproul defines humanism as an anthropocentric (man-centered) view of life as opposed to a theocentric (God-centered) view of life.[20] He traces its origins to the pre-Socratic Greek philosopher Protagoras, whose motto was *homo mensura,* meaning "man (is) the measure." Thus, humanism views man as the ultimate measure of all things. As a result of its own presuppositions, humanism rejects the concept of divinely revealed moral absolutes and argues for man's right to determine his own morality.

Modern humanism, as reflected in the *Humanist Manifestos* (1933, 1973) and the *Humanist Declaration* (1980), is decidedly anti-Christian in its bias. One leading proponent of humanist education, John Dewey, said, "Religion tends to hinder the evolutionary progress of man."[21] In reality, Francis Schaeffer contended, humanism borrowed the moral concerns of Christianity and tore them loose from their theological foundation. Unless it is stopped, he warned, humanism "intends to beat to death the [Christian] base which made our culture possible."[22]

THE FILTRATION OF IDEAS

The present conflict between religion and politics is not merely a political issue. Rather, it is the last wave of the conflict which has been raging between Christianity and secularism throughout this century. The first waves of this conflict were philosophical and then theological. As the philosophies of relativism and secularism began to dominate thinking in the late nineteenth century, they soon influenced theology as well. This gave rise to theological liberalism and the eventual ecclesiastical controversies between fundamentalism and modernism.[23]

As the concepts of relativism and secularism gained control of institutionalized religion, they provoked theological debate which, in turn, led to ecclesiastical power struggles to control the ideology of the mainline denominations. Thus the argumentation shifted to the issue of ecclesiastical control. When conservatives were unable to prevent liberalism from infiltrating and eventually controlling the theological institutions, they withdrew, forming new denominations and new institutions. This left liberalism entrenched in the mainline institutions. As time passed, succeeding generations of theological students became increasingly secularized so that today one cannot distinguish a liberal theological agenda from a secular one.

The influence of nearly a century of liberal preaching has now filtered down to the level of the common person in society. Popular literature, television, and movies all tend to reflect this mentality. As the liberal mind-set gained a grip on society, it also influenced the political process through legislative and judicial change. Thus political decisions began to reflect the values of secularism.

This process of the filtration of ideas was first brought to the attention of evangelicals by the late Francis Schaeffer.[24] He viewed philosophy as the wellspring from which popular culture derived. As philosophical concepts filter down through the culture, they first affect the elite and eventually become popularized by society in general. The process works something like this:

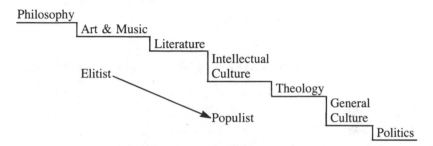

Filtration of Ideas: From Intellectual Elites
to Popular Culture to Politics.

Schaeffer argued that the philosophical concepts of Kant and Hegel gave rise to a whole new way of thinking that resulted in relativism. He suggested that this concept spread geographically from Germany to Holland and Switzerland before it caught on in England and America. As an American living in Switzerland, Schaeffer realized that American culture was moving in the same direction, though at a slower pace, as European culture. God was simply being eliminated as a serious intellectual option. Schaeffer also observed that relativism affected the intellectual classes first and was passed on to the workers by the mass media, bypassing the middle class. He observed, "The middle class was not touched by it and often is still not touched by it."[25]

It is our observation that the strength of the middle-class evangelical church in America is our greatest deterrent to relativism and secularism. Were it not for the thousands of evangelical churches representing millions of members, secularism would have swept America long ago. This is why there is still a great void between evangelical and liberal churches today. Not only does our theology differ, but our entire response to modernity rests upon totally different philosophical foundations.

What is unique about the twentieth century, however, is the ability of the mass media to translate secular values to every level of society through television, films, books, and magazines. Our inability to think critically and objectively while being entertained, especially by television, movies, or videos, leaves even the Christian community vulnerable to the influence of secularism. We can watch a program that challenges or contradicts the very values we hold dear and never even realize it!

POLITICS: CHRISTIANITY'S LAST STAND

The grip of secularism on our society is so tight that its influence is being felt in nearly every area of American life. The secularization of education, morality, and public policy eventually results in the politicization of those beliefs through the legislative and judicial process. The end result will be the legalization of secularism and the disenfranchisement of Judeo-Christianity.

Politics, in the broadest sense of human governance, is the last line of defense for religion in our society. The filtration of secularism is now so nearly complete that it dares to enshrine itself through the political processes. For example, when evolutionists argued for academic freedom to present the theory of evolution in the public schools at the time of the Scopes Trial in 1925, it was assumed by both sides in the debate that creationism would also be allowed to be taught. In fact, that assumption was so widely held that no one seriously questioned it. All the evolutionists wanted at that time was the opportunity to gain a fair hearing for their position. But in the decades that passed, secularism gained such control of public education that the teaching of creation is now forbidden by law. Creationists do not even have the same fundamental academic freedom for which evolutionists once begged.[26]

A more recent example of the controversy between secularism and religion was the Civil Rights Restoration Act of 1987, popularly known as the Grove City bill. The issue involved the right of Grove City College, an evangelical Presbyterian institution, to dismiss a homosexual staff member for violation of the church school's code of moral conduct. When initial attempts to pass the bill failed, liberal members of Congress attached it to other proposed legislation and President Reagan vetoed it.

In the controversy that resulted, the Congress was pressured by various religious organizations headed by Jerry Falwell, James Kennedy, Tim LaHaye, and James Dobson to support the president's veto. In reaction, the American Civil Liberties Union (ACLU) and Norman Lear's People for the American Way took out full-page advertisements in major newspapers and lobbied the Congress to override the veto, which they did.

Evangelicals opposed the bill because they believed it was an attempt by secularists to force non-Christian morality on the Christian community. Ironically, the ads run against this evangelical backlash implied just the opposite! Since the bill forbid the use of federal funds to institutions that "discriminated" against women, minorities, and homosexuals, the secularists actually criticized the Christians for trying to use federal funds to finance their intolerance, when that was not the reason for the evangelical reaction at all. They were trying to get the secularists to leave them alone.

One of the peculiarities of a democracy is that it is always in a state of flux. Any particular group can potentially propose new legislation at any time. Therefore, democracies are rarely static. There is nearly always a state of fluidity in the exchange of ideas. Unfortunately, most Christians tend to forget this. We think that things will continue as they have always been. As a result, we live in a naive moment of false security in which we have forgotten the whole history of the world!

A PUBLICLY IRRELEVANT FAITH

While acknowledging his personal concerns about the illusion of political power brokering, Charles Colson admits that we have come to a time when many people are advocating a privately engaging but publicly irrelevant faith.[27] He argues that two extreme positions dominate Christian thinking on the issue of religion and politics. On the one hand, he sees a *politicized faith* which tends to seek political solutions to spiritual problems while neglecting the Church's real spiritual mission. In this regard, Colson criticizes the New Right for falling into the same trap as the liberal mainline denominations, which have been overtly political since the 1960s. On the other hand, Colson observes a *privatized faith* which "divorces religious and spiritual beliefs from public actions."[28]

Colson observes that the political left, including mainline religion, has a "morbid fear of religion encroaching on the secular realm."[29] We would add that the New Right has an equally morbid fear of secularism encroaching on religious freedoms. This is exactly where the controversy between religion and secularism lies today. While mainline religion has an innate fear of imposing religious values in a pluralistic society, evangelicals have an innate fear of allowing secularists to impose antireligious values on that society.

Colson criticizes New York Governor Mario Cuomo for a publicly irrelevant position on abortion. Colson notes that the governor is a practicing Catholic who holds to his church's belief that abortion is wrong. As a public official, Cuomo acknowledged in a speech at the University of Notre Dame in 1984 that he not only could not impose his views on others, but that he was under no obligation to advocate such views either. Such a position, Colson says, is "impotent to reverse the tides of secularism."[30]

Where do the extremes of privatization or politicization leave us? Unfortunately, they tend to leave us in confusion. On the one extreme are Christians who believe we must take over the government in order to enforce religious values. On the other extreme are Christians who pietistically want to avoid all public or political issues. We believe that the Church can have a proper balance between these two extremes. We must become a voice of conscience to our society or forever forfeit any spiritual influence in matters of public policy. The fact that religious, spiritual, and moral issues have become a subject of political debate simply indicates how far secularism has already advanced in our society.

DRAWING A LINE OF DEFENSE

Much of the New Right involvement in political issues has been little more than drawing a line of defense against the encroachment of secularism. For the most part, the New Right has not advocated taking rights away from secularists or humanists. Conservatives have merely insisted that secularists not deny their rights to live by the moral values and principles they believe to be valid. For example, the New Right is not calling for the elimination of existing rights for anyone. They simply oppose extending those rights to include the imposition of a nonbiblical morality upon the Church or church-related institutions.

If we do not draw a line of defense at this point of the debate, we will end up sacrificing everything we believe in the area of public policy. This does not mean that the Church cannot survive in a hostile society. In some cases, as in ancient pagan Rome and modern atheistic communism, true Christianity has actually flourished. However, in other cases, such as under the sword of Islam, it has been eradicated.

Conservatives are merely calling the Church to awaken to its responsibilities in this latter part of the twentieth century. There is no excuse for us to lose our religious freedoms in a democratic society. If this does happen, we will have no one to blame but ourselves. The irrelevance of a privatized pietism is as dangerous to the health of Christianity as is the apathy of a self-indulgent Church.

Whether we like it or not, we have come to religion's last stand in American culture. The political debate is the final attempt of secularism to prevail over religion in our society. The implications of this debate have eternal consequences. For secularism, all human values must be understood in the present, whereas the biblical worldview is eternal. R. C. Sproul rightly observes, "This is precisely where Christianity and secularism collide. This is the point of conflict."[31] Sproul observes that "right now" counts forever in Christianity. What we do has eternal significance because our existence is related to God Himself.

THE DEATH OF GOD AND THE DEATH OF MAN

At the peak of secularization in the 1960s and 1970s, theologians began to talk about synthesizing Christianity with secularism in the concept of the death of God. They viewed God as having surrendered His transcendence and capitulating to the secular through the incarnation of Christ. When Jesus took on humanity, the transcendent God "died," they argued, leaving mankind with the pursuit of its own solutions to its problems.[32]

Sproul again observes, "The death of God, in terms of the loss of transcendence and the loss of the eternal, also means the death of man. It means that history has no transcendent goal. There is no eternal purpose."[33] Once the secular mind-set gains control of the way a society thinks, it will not be long until those thoughts are translated into political structures.

In a perceptive article entitled, "The Drift Away from Life," Truman Dollar observed that society is losing its belief in the sanctity of life. He remarks, "For most of human history the law has leaned on the side that life is worth preserving. That view is now shifting, and we are moving toward the idea that a substantial number of people are better off dead."[34] He observes that certain changes and practices in our society related to the rejection of Creation have "created a moral climate that is supportive of the move away from a high view of life."

In a dramatic courtroom scene in the television version of Jerome Laurence's *Inherit the Wind,* which was based on the famous Scopes Trial, the lawyer for the defense asks a young student whose teacher had taught him evolution, "Did evolution ever do you any harm?" The lawyer asks the boy about his general health and his ability to play baseball, implying that this belief has in no way damaged the young man. While it is true that such a belief may not affect one's athletic ability, it has in time damaged the entire fabric of our society.

Os Guinness has observed that if man is merely an animal, he may just as well live like one.[35] He states that modern man's view of himself in terms of his moral behavior irretrievably alters his view of reality. "Anything left of contemporary concepts of morality and identity will be reduced to the level of the illusory, and the implications for individuals and for civilization are far-reaching."[36] Fifteen years ago, Guinness warned that man was headed into a period of alienation, followed by mystification and romanticism. He pointed to Nietzsche's view that man is in an "ontological predicament," like being tied by a rope over an abyss. He is caught in an

106

impossible struggle that results in "the great seasickness" of a world without God.[37]

It was this concept from Nietzsche that led the French existentialist Jean Paul Sartre to call his first novel *Nausea*. In it, Sartre concluded, "Every existent is born without reason, prolongs itself out of weakness and dies by chance." Thus, Sartre saw life as a "fundamental absurdity" without God.[38]

When man faces the awfulness of naked secularism, Guinness argues, he retreats into a psychological mystification by which he arbitrarily attempts to assign meaning to his life by establishing norms of behavior by the consensus of the population. The end result of this process is the legitimization of one man's abnormality as freedom from another man's normality. An extreme example of this is found in the Soviet Union, when those criticizing society are sent to mental asylums for "paranoid delusions about reforming society."[39] One such accused geneticist, Zhores Medvedev, said, "If things go on like this, it will end with healthy, sane people sitting in mad houses, while dangerous mental cases will walk about freely."[40]

The final stage of the decline of Western thought is romanticism. This occurs when we give up the aspirations of a Judeo-Christian worldview and begin to romanticize the consequences. For example, when Judeo-Christian views of death, dying, and eternal life are eliminated, secularists begin romanticizing a pragmatic and casual approach to death as the ultimate escape. Guinness also warned that this would eventually lead to a revival of the concept of reincarnation as modern man's ultimate attempt to escape the meaninglessness of nonbeing.[41]

THE NEW AGE RAGE

Modern man has reached the point where he does not want to face the logical consequences of a secular world without God. But instead of repenting of his rebellion against God, he is now turning to a kind of scientific mysticism that has been popularized as the New Age movement.[42] Modern New Age mysticism is a combination of transcendentalism, spiritualism, oriental mysticism, and transpersonal psychology.[43] It rests upon the humanist psychology of

Abraham Maslow, Fritz Perls, Carl Rogers, and Rollo May, all of whom emphasized the elevation of personal growth as the highest good and placed the transcendent at the top of the list of man's hierarchical needs.[44]

The New Psychology, as it came to be called, developed a trend in therapy toward deification of the isolated self and the rejection of traditional morality as selfishness and moral blindness in favor of holistic psychic health. Thus, it developed hand-in-hand with the whole Human Potential movement. Key elements of New Age thought include restructuring the mind through meditation, sensory deprivation (for example, flotation therapy), and the self-tuning of the mind and body to become receptors and transmitters of cosmic forces. Psychic therapies claim to manipulate "life energies" to provide inner healing of individuals and to promote human relationships in harmony with cosmic forces.

Dave Hunt's *The Seduction of Christianity* undoubtedly goes to extremes to combat the infiltration of New Age thinking in the Church, but he is certainly correct in his observation that the whole of New Age mysticism is based upon Teilhard de Chardin's concept of the evolution of the soul.[45] Teilhard was a French Catholic priest, paleontologist, and theologian who attempted to "Christianize" evolution with a theistic view in which the soul emerged as the driving force of evolution. This evolution would lead to a collective superconsciousness of humanity, which in turn would result in a new age of life on earth.[46]

Teilhard's mysticism is expressed most clearly in his now popular *Hymn of the Universe,* in which he advocated the concept of centrism, or the tendency of things to converge and move to the center, resulting in the totalization of all phenomena.[47] This end result of spiritual evolution will be realized in a collectivism of all reality, by which everything will become a part of a new organic whole. Present human consciousness (*noosphere*) will culminate in a *theosphere,* when converging human spirits transcend matter and space in a mystical union called the *omega point.*[48]

It is this merging of scientific mysticism with a rejection of materialistic secularism which has resulted in New Age thinking. New Age thinking then couples with the Human Potential movement, which offers a number of techniques to advance one's metaphysical evolution.[49] Since all ideas have political consequences, we should not be surprised to discover that the political agenda of New Age thinking includes ecological concerns, sexual equality, and the unification of the world order by the transformation of the current political order through a "planetary consciousness."[50]

Like the Christian reconstructionists, the New Age transformationalists seek the total transformation of society along ideological lines consistent with its own beliefs. By challenging the "myths" of matter, time, space, and death, New Agers believe they will release our untapped human potential to create a new and better world.[51]

The great danger is that the unbalanced concerns of New Age mystics and Christian pietists will leave both groups divorced from any serious attempt to influence public policy, allowing raw secularists complete control of the public policy formation of American life. Both extremes represent the final and fatal efforts of modern man to avoid any responsible action in light of the advance of naked secularism. Thus, the process of mystification is completed and man remains helpless to deal with reality.

THE PRESENT DILEMMA:
THE NEED FOR HOPE

Twentieth-century man has come to the ultimate conclusion that he needs hope beyond himself to solve the problems of life. His choices are relatively few indeed. He can turn to God, himself, others, nature, or a mystic collective consciousness, but in reality he only has two choices: himself or God. Ironically, man's rationalism has driven him to irrationality. Either he must accept the logical consequences of living in a world without God or he must turn to God. All other options are merely wishful thinking.

Modern Americans, however, usually find it difficult to throw God away altogether. We always seem to rely on some popular myth that Superman (or someone like him) is going to come from outer space to save the world. Unfortunately, our own scientific rationality ought to tell us that this isn't so. The blatant secularist knows it isn't so and has to admit that man must solve his problems alone.

The great cause for despair in Western culture is the stark realization that man may well be closer to destroying himself than to solving his problems. Everyone born after Hiroshima knows the great horror of living in a world that could be destroyed by the very technology that has made it great. This reality lurks in the subconscious of everyone in our society. But it represents such an ugly reality that we psychologically suppress it and blank it out. In the meantime, we make nearly every decision in light of that subconscious truth.

AN AGENDA FOR THE NEXT CENTURY

There are many issues in our contemporary culture which the Church must address as it faces the twenty-first century. Many of these issues loom as large as life itself. Most of them have serious moral, ethical, and spiritual connotations. And whether we like it or not, most of them are politically related issues. These must be addressed if we are to have any real hope for the future.

1. Freedom.   Freedom is one of the fundamental human rights guaranteed by the American Constitution. Without freedom it is debatable whether life is really worth living. Emblazoned across the Liberty Bell is the biblical quotation, ''Proclaim liberty throughout all the land unto all the inhabitants thereof'' (Leviticus 25:10). Liberty is the great heritage of the American people. It needs to be protected and extended to all peoples. The Scripture reminds us, ''. . . where the Spirit of the Lord is, there is liberty'' (2 Corinthians 3:17).

Though liberty is the ultimate freedom, it is a freedom that must be maintained. James Madison once asked, ''But what is government itself but the greatest of all reflections on human nature? If men were angels, no government would be necessary.''[52] Christians especially understand this concept because of their strong belief in the depravity of man. If we don't protect our freedom, someone will eventually take it away.

2. Life.   The right to life is the most fundamental freedom of all. Without life there can be no freedom. Evangelical Christians view man as the unique creation of God who alone bears His image (*see* Genesis 1:27). We take a high view of human life as a gift from

110

God. In referring to God's creation of man, the Scripture says, "For thou hast made him a little lower than the angels, and hast crowned him with glory and honour" (Psalms 8:5).

If man is nothing more than an animal, his value and worth are relative. An individual human being may be sacrificed for the common good, or an unwanted child may be aborted because he or she is inconvenient, expensive, or undesirable. John Eidsmoe correctly observes that the "unborn child is a human being, therefore, killing him constitutes the killing of a human being."[53] We cannot expect God's blessing on our lives or our nation if we allow this genocide to continue. Stopping abortion, euthanasia, and infanticide is the only way to protect the dignity of human life for future generations.

3. Peace. Peace is the ultimate ingredient to sustaining life and freedom. We cannot assume that it will always be there unless we protect it. There is a great deal of debate within the Christian community as to how that should be accomplished. Some favor nuclear disarmament as the best deterrent. But all of us should favor peace as our ultimate objective. Our Lord Himself said, "Blessed are the peacemakers . . ." (Matthew 5:9).

The tragic consequences of war in this century should alert us all to the irrationality of global violence. Yet it may well be again that we will have to protect the peace from enemy aggressors. We must be ready to do so if necessary, while constantly working to avoid such action if possible. The Scripture encourages us, ". . . Be at peace among yourselves" (1 Thessalonians 5:13) and to follow after ". . . peace, with them that call on the Lord out of a pure heart" (2 Timothy 2:22).

4. Biblical Values. Virtually every controversy between religion and secularism boils down to the conflict over biblical values. Once we get beyond the discussion of what principles and values are taught in Scripture, we are faced with the issue of obedience to those principles and acceptance of those values. This is and always will be the crux of the argument between Judeo-Christian religion and secularism. We will probably always be divided over issues of family, life, education, pornography, abortion, sex, marriage, crime, and punishment.

111

Christians cannot hope to influence the world for Christ by abandoning their Christian principles. John Stott has said, "There is a serious dearth of leaders in the contemporary world." He observes that "technical know-how abounds, but wisdom is in short supply." To counter this situation, Stott recommends five essential ingredients for effective leadership:

1. *Vision:* The imaginative perception that combines insight and foresight, compounded with a deep dissatisfaction with what *is* and a clear grasp of what *could be.*
2. *Industry:* The willingness to turn dreams into plans and hard work in order to accomplish your goals.
3. *Perseverance:* The willingness to sacrifice all that is necessary to overcome the opposition to your dreams and plans, and bring them to fruition.
4. *Service:* The ultimate recognition of the value of others is the willingness to serve them as an expression of one's obedience to God.
5. *Discipline:* The self-denial necessary to keep going when zest degenerates into drudgery. This is the essential ingredient to keeping the vision alive.[54]

5. *Spiritual Revival.* More than anything else we need a genuine spiritual revival if we are to affect the world for Christ in the century ahead. There is no place for hypocrisy which breaks the link between belief and behavior. We need to learn to live our faith in such a powerful and positive way that we can stand up to public scrutiny that wants to know if we are for real.

The ingredients of revival are the same as they have always been. We need a genuine repentance based upon biblical truth, empowered by a visitation of the Spirit of God. Such a revival must supersede the emotional hype of current televangelism, and it must produce a genuine conviction of sin far greater than that of typical renewal movements.

True revival must arise from judgment beginning at the house of God. It must result in the eventual transformation of society by transforming the lives of individuals apart from political structures. Only then can a transformed Church offer hope to society that can be translated into political action.

Chapter Seven

Evangelical Alternatives: Can We Really Stay Out of Politics?

For which of you . . . sitteth not down first, and counteth the cost. . . .

Luke 14:28

 It has become trendy to talk about Christians staying out of politics.[1] Some have tired of all the attention the subject has been given, and others fear that such attention has militated against the Church's ultimate goals of evangelism and discipleship. Certainly it has been unfortunate that more has been written in the last ten years about evangelicals in politics than has been written about anything else they believe or practice.

However, not all evangelicals share this concern. "At least they are talking about us," Jerry Falwell has said more than once. "That's better than it used to be!"[2] Others, like Tim LaHaye, have argued that evangelicals have just begun to make a difference and that this is no time to give up the fight. LaHaye recently said, "One lesson we've learned in the past ten years is that if we give in to the pacifism that has been our tradition since the pietistic movement, we will be steam-rolled by the secular-humanist juggernaut that is determined to secularize public policy."[3]

POLITICS AND PUBLIC POLICY

Any serious discussion of evangelical options needs to begin with a few basic observations about the nature of politics and the forma-

113

tion of public policy. If politics in the broadest sense of the term is the process of human beings living in community, and in the narrow sense is the science of government, then we are faced with the inevitability of fallible humans governing fallible humans.[4]

Politics becomes a process of establishing, and in most cases legalizing, certain behavior. This is generally done in regard to (1) belief in an absolute or divine law; (2) the consensus of the majority; or (3) the forceful imposition of a totalitarian standard. In any political system, certain laws are established as a code of conduct for society. It is utter foolishness for people to argue against the imposition of morality by law. All law is the imposition on society of someone's beliefs, whether they claim those beliefs to be rooted in God, in people, or in the State.[5]

This issue has been greatly misunderstood in the debate on religion and politics. The very people who are usually complaining that evangelicals are trying to impose their beliefs on the rest of society are doing the very same thing themselves! In fact, it was the threat of such imposition of secular beliefs that caused the evangelical backlash in the first place.[6]

The time has come for both sides to honestly admit that they are trying to implement their viewpoint because they believe it is right. The secularist fears a religiously dominated society in which personal freedoms are limited by religious beliefs. The religionist fears a secularist-dominated society in which all religious values are stripped away, leaving society vulnerable to antireligious bias.[7]

THE GENIUS OF DEMOCRACY

In a very real sense, the two extremes of religion and secularism form a corrective within a pluralistic democratic society. The one checks and balances the other. It is no more fair to ask a Christian to cease being a Christian in his approach to society than it would be to ask a secularist to cease being secular in his approach.

This is ultimately the genius of democracy. It provides for an open debate on all issues on the basis of moral persuasion. Neither side can outlaw the other without convincing the other of the legitimacy of its viewpoint. While this is no easy task, it prevents extremists from either camp gaining easy sway over the general public. Thus the two provisions of the First Amendment regarding the federal government neither establishing a state religion nor prohibiting the free exercise of religion are both protected.

While this process of moral suasion is not a simple one, it is the area where evangelicals potentially can make their greatest contribution.[8] It is one thing for evangelical preachers to tell their own congregations that they have the answers to the world's problems, but it is another thing to put those answers up to public scrutiny. However, as we do so we can both refine our position and state our case to the public more effectively.

THE NECESSITY OF INVOLVEMENT

While there are certainly potential dangers in political involvement, including both the seduction and illusion of power, there is also the compelling necessity of our involvement. "Failure to do so," writes Richard Neuhaus, "results in the abandonment of our responsibility to care for the world that is the object of God's creating and preserving love." He argues that culture formation and politics are among the ways in which Christians are called to serve their neighbors. "When politics is conceived as a salvific project," he warns, "it is indeed a lethal illusion. But more modestly understood as the task of preventing injustice and maybe even achieving a modicum of justice, political engagement can be for the Christian a form of discipleship."[9]

John Stott adds the compelling analysis that evangelicals tend to want to drop out of the political process every time the going gets tough. He blames this on two factors. First, he argues that many Christians have such an other-worldly orientation that they become indifferent to social injustice as long as it doesn't affect them personally. These "irresponsible escapists," as he calls them, are the modern equivalent of ancient mystics pietistically hiding in monasteries while the rest of the world is in chaos. Second, he accuses some American evangelicals of being so success-oriented that they bail out of every cause they think they can't win.[10]

Evangelical Christians were socially and politically active in the eighteenth and nineteenth centuries. Today's evangelicals are quick to point to them with pride because of their successful opposition to slavery, child labor abuses, and the plight of the insane. We are quick to acknowledge their influence in producing legislative reform that brought social and educational opportunities for the poor. But we dare not think these changes came easily or without great personal sacrifice.[11]

By contrast, we must look with shame on the many German evangelical Christians who failed to speak up during the Nazi extermination of 6 million Jews.[12] While there were certainly individual dissenting voices, the evangelicals never spoke up officially to protest the Aryan legislation or the anti-Jewish discrimination it brought about. Think what could have been accomplished for Jewish-Christian relations if hundreds of evangelical Germans had put their lives on the line for the Jews! Think of the testimony for true Christianity had evangelicals been willing to protest and, if necessary, even die for justice in the case of the Jews. In all likelihood, the willingness of Germans to die for Jews would have brought an outcry from the German people which could have prevented the Holocaust.

After the Second World War, German evangelicals issued the Stuttgart Declaration in which they could only apologize, "It is to our self-indictment that we have not made a more courageous confession."[13] A great injustice had been done and the Church sat by and watched. But before American evangelicals criticize others, we must ask ourselves what we are doing to counter the great injustices of our own time.

The abortion of over 20 million unborn babies in America is the greatest injustice of our day and demands our response, lest we have to issue our own apology in the future. It is in issues like abortion that theology, ethics, and politics converge. They are not merely separate academic disciplines. They are convergent expressions of how one's theology affects one's life and practice.

Thus, Stott appeals for more and better Christian involvement in politics, not less. He writes, "There is a great need for more Christian thinkers in contemporary society, who will throw themselves into the public debate, and for more Christian activists who

will organize pressure groups to promote the work of persuasion.''
He calls for men and women who will be ''thoroughly Christian''
and make ''no attempt to conceal the origins of their concern.''[14]
We believe that his balanced concern for Christian involvement in
society based upon zeal for God and love for mankind is absolutely
correct.

IMPOSSIBILITY OF NEUTRALITY

William Willimon, chaplain of Duke University, has raised the
issue of political neutrality in relation to what he calls the ''chains
of religious freedom.''[15] He argues that a purely secularized democracy offers us religious freedom only so far as we are willing to
keep our public mouths shut. He writes, ''We enjoy freedom to be
Jewish or Christian here as long as we keep our religion to ourselves
and let the government handle public matters.'' He goes on to argue
that the Church must be willing to speak out against moral wrong
whether our message offends the secular mind-set or not.

''Observers of our national moral decay call for a restored religious underpinning of our national ideals,'' Willimon adds. ''At the
same time they want the state to be 'completely neutral.' But how
would Christians set out to provide moral underpinning apart from
their commitment to Jesus Christ, which can hardly be described as
neutral?''[16]

The time has come for evangelicals to speak as prophets of God
to the great evils of our society. We cannot keep quiet on the flimsy
excuse that we don't want to appear excessive or hypocritical. Our
agenda must be refined in light of the moral and political debate. We
must prioritize that agenda to give the greatest attention to the
greatest needs. If we really believe that abortion is murder, we must
cry out against it until it stops! Cal Thomas has rightly argued that
this is our single greatest national sin and it cannot play second
fiddle to the issue of whether the United States ought to flag oil
tankers in the Persian Gulf![17]

THE NAKED PUBLIC SQUARE

In many ways politics has become our last line of defense against
the legal enshrinement of raw secularism. It is no secret that Amer-

ican society has become increasingly secularized throughout the twentieth century. As secularism gained an ever-increasing grip on the intellectual life of America, it should have been obvious that it would eventually seek to impose its beliefs by political legislation. Thus, in this process, politics becomes the final expression of the beliefs of those involved. Just as the founders of America sought to give politics a religious and moral vision, so the secularizers of America have sought to give it a secular vision.[18]

R. C. Sproul has rightly oberved, "Students of history realize that no society can survive, no civilization can function, without some unifying system of thought."[19] This unifying system generally takes the form of a philosophy, religion, myth, or political system to which society becomes devoted. America has always been an unusual combination of both a religious and political system. From the Pilgrims on the *Mayflower,* who came to America "for the Glory of God and the advancement of the Christian faith," to the candidacy of George Bush, who recently told the National Religious Broadcasters, "I have not come to ask for your votes, but for your prayers," religion has always played a vital part in American public life.[20]

British historian Paul Johnson has observed, "The political culture of the United States is strongly religious" because of the "harmony of religion and liberty." He explains that religion has always been the champion of liberty in America and, therefore, there is no conflict between the religious establishment and the political process. Indeed, he argues that the influence of religion in America can be traced back to the Puritans like Jonathan Edwards, who saw religion as the unifying force in American society.[21]

Richard Neuhaus has argued very effectively that religion and democracy can indeed coexist. However, he observes that the current trend in American society toward overt secularization leaves the square of public policy naked of the very values upon which it was established. "To be truly democratic and to endure," he writes, "such a public policy must be grounded in values that are based in Judeo-Christian religion."[22] He argues that evangelicals have foolishly avoided social and political involvement, naively assuming that someone else would shape public policy in their best interests.

"Attention must be paid to the political," Neuhaus asserts, "not because everything is political, but because, if attention is not paid, the political threatens to encompass everything."[23]

This is the problem that brought evangelicals and fundamentalists into politics in the first place. The vast majority of them have never called for the establishment of a theocracy. Most of them are not even calling for a reconstruction of the American legal system. They simply want the secularists to leave the system alone. But in the meantime, they do not intend to sit idly by and watch secularists reconstruct America into an antireligious state. They are especially outraged over government regulation of sexual and family values.[24]

Evangelical Christians believe that American public policy should reflect our nation's biblical and moral heritage. If it does not, most evangelicals hope that at least it will not undermine that legacy. In other words, when a political or judicial decision is made that reflects antireligious beliefs, evangelicals take it personally as an affront to their beliefs. It is only natural that they would react against such policies.

Neuhaus has observed that fundamentalists and evangelicals have often been guilty of perpetuating the naked public square by refusing to enter the public policy debate. Thus, Neuhaus argues, the separation of private belief from public policy actually allows secularism to spread unchecked.[25] He also observes that the rise of Moral Majority "kicked a tripwire" alerting the American public to the fact that values and morality are inseparably linked. We cannot have a moral society and a value-free society at the same time. In other words, as secularism prevails in a society, traditional values begin to disappear.

THE BANKRUPTCY OF LIBERALISM

One of the major problems in American religion has been the nearly total capitulation of liberal mainline religion to the secular agenda. In what Neuhaus calls the Great Accommodation, the "prophets" of liberalism became pacifiers of secularism and left religion "bereft of its miraculous and transcendent quality."[26] Many have begun to question whether the mainline Protestant

119

churches have an agenda of their own.[27] Others have observed that the liberal churches' adherence to the social gospel was a kind of left-wing "reconstructionism."[28] For example, Walter Rauschenbusch, the father of the social gospel movement, said the "essential purpose of Christianity is to transform human society into the Kingdom of God." He urged Christians to lead the way in establishing the Kingdom of God on earth by the transformation of the political and legal structure. Thus, he proposed a reconstruction of human society by the transformation of its social structures.[29]

Unfortunately, the popular reception of the social gospel concept by the mainline churches shifted their emphasis from evangelism to social concern. In time, the liberal wing of the Church allied itself almost totally with left-wing political stances. In reaction to both the liberal theology and liberal politics of the mainline churches, fundamentalists and evangelicals shifted more dramatically toward the right. Eventually, the two camps of American Protestantism became polarized on virtually every issue.

The first public clash between liberals and conservatives came in the fundamentalist versus modernist controversies of the 1920s.[30] The liberal wing of the Church wanted to "modernize" its theology to accommodate rationalism, higher criticism, evolution, and the social gospel. To do so, the liberals openly questioned the inspiration of the Bible, the deity of Christ, the necessity of His death as an atonement for sin, His literal resurrection from the dead, and a host of other doctrines. By the second decade of the twentieth century, liberalism was entrenched in the major Protestant denominations.[31]

Conservative Protestants reacted by affirming the doctrines the liberals were denying and identifying them as the "fundamentals" of the Christian faith. Inevitably, the two factions moved toward a head-on collision. When J. Gresham Machen led a group of conservative professors and students to withdraw from Princeton Seminary and the United Presbyterian Church in 1929, he set off a chain reaction of separatism that led to a dozen such withdrawals.[32] In the name of doctrinal purity, the fundamentalists withdrew from the mainline denominations and formed their own denominations, fellowships, and associations. They established their own schools and missionary societies and began functioning as though the parent denominations no longer existed.

With the fundamentalists temporarily out of the way, liberalism reached its apex during the 1930s and 1940s. It was generally assumed that they had won the ecclesiastical war with fundamentalism and that the latter had retreated to somewhere in Appalachia! The liberal clergy had a heyday dominating the media in both radio and television from 1930 to 1960. During this time, conservatives were forced to buy air time on commercial stations. However, this eventually led to the expansion of radio ministries by popular speakers such as Charles E. Fuller, M. R. DeHaan, and Donald Grey Barnhouse, who attracted large followings.[33]

Like the hare racing the tortoise, the mainline churches falsely assumed that they had the race won and began to rest on their laurels. However, they were lacking a crucial ingredient which was a reflection of their defective theology—evangelism! They made virtually no effort to win new converts to their beliefs. As a result, they began to decline numerically. It was not until the late 1960s that it became apparent that liberals were losing their influence in American society. But today that decline has become a toboggan slide to oblivion. At the rate the mainline churches are losing members, they are in danger of going out of existence by the middle of the next century.[34]

That calamity contains a somber warning to conservative Christians. We could also be in danger of hitching our theology to a particular political position that could result more in the politicizing of Christianity than in the Christianizing of politics. Charles Colson has warned: "Today's misspent enthusiasm for political solutions to the moral problems of our culture arises from . . . too low a view of the power of a sovereign God and too high a view of the ability of man."[35]

PHENOMENAL GROWTH OF THE
EVANGELICAL CHURCH

The controversy with liberalism forced the evangelicals to start building the Church in America all over again. As they withdrew from the mainline churches, evangelicals and fundamentalists caught fire with a renewed fervency for preaching and evangelism. Despite their own divisions and ecclesiastical infighting, they began growing by leaps and bounds. That growth has spawned thousands of new churches reaching millions of people with the Gospel of new life in Christ.[36]

As the twentieth century progressed, conservative Protestants basically fell into three camps: fundamentalists, evangelicals, or charismatics. *Fundamentalists* have often been described as militant separatists. This movement has especially appealed to blue-collar Christians. They place a strong emphasis on confrontational preaching, aggressive evangelism, and strict separatism from liberal denominational associations.[37] *Evangelicals* have generally been described as moderate conservatives whose appeal is greatest among white-collar Christians. They place a strong emphasis on teaching, worship, and personal relationships.[38] *Charismatics* are Pentecostals who place a strong emphasis on the baptism of the Holy Spirit, tongues, and healing. They hold to a basic evangelical theology of Christ and salvation but differ from the other two groups in their emphasis on spiritual gifts (Greek, *charismata*).[39]

While great differences of theology, ministry, and worship exist between these three wings of the conservative Church, they are all committed to evangelism. In their own way and style, each of these groups has won millions of converts to Christ from America's unchurched population and from within the ranks of the mainline churches.

During the fifty years from 1930 to 1980, these groups were growing unnoticed by the general public. They had little influence on American politics or public policy. They were not viewed as a threat to anyone; in fact, they were virtually ignored by the secular media. When they burst on the scene publicly in the late 1970s and early 1980s, the secular press was at a loss to explain where they had come from and what they wanted.[40]

Since the television evangelists were the most visible to the general public and since one of them, Jerry Falwell, had galvanized a portion of them into a political lobby known as Moral Majority, the media assumed that they were a monolithic voting bloc that had emerged out of the New South. To this day, the public opinion is that all three groups are one and the same. That is why the moral failures of charismatic preachers Jim Bakker and Jimmy Swaggart are hung around the neck of all televangelists and all born again Christians. Their problems have often been cited for the failure of Pat Robertson's presidential bid, though neither was actively involved in his campaign.[41]

Unfortunately, conservative Christians have a habit of trying to dissociate themselves from embarrassment. The tragic events of recent years have already begun to polarize people within the conservative camp. There are those who feel that all this political involvement has been a waste of time and money.[42] Some feel that Christian political concerns are amateurish and naive, and that the Church's political opinions reflect nothing more than the "moral and political idealism of the surrounding culture."[43] Others feel that we must rethink, refine, and reshape our political focus in the light of what we have learned in recent years.[44] Still others are calling for a greater involvement based on the fact that we are just beginning to make a difference.[45]

WHAT HAVE WE LEARNED?

The years of socio-political involvement for evangelicals have not been easy ones. Early victories, self-proclaimed successes, and euphoric triumphalism have given way to a more serious assessment of the reality of long-term political involvement. It is to be hoped that we have now realized that there are no shortcuts to success and no simple solutions to our national problems. Future endeavors are going to need to be carefully weighed and evaluated. Specific priorities for our efforts need to be established in the areas where we can do the most good.

By now, we should also have learned that we can make a difference in the public policy formation of this country if we will be patient with the democratic process. We may not be able to change things overnight, but we have gotten the attention of the nation. No longer can politicians simply dismiss us as an irrelevant minority. Forty to fifty million professing born again Christians are a sizable portion of the population. We can make our voice heard and we can make a difference in our national life.

Having been involved in the earliest stages of the New Right's formation, we believe there are five key issues to be resolved if we are to be successful in any future political involvement. Our list is not exhaustive, but we believe it is crucial to the future of evangelical influence in American politics.

1. Private Morality versus Public Policy. A recurring tension in the debate on religion and politics involves the relationship between private moral/religious beliefs and the establishment of public policy.[46] It is generally accepted that the basic laws of our society rest upon a Judeo-Christian foundation as it was shaped and passed on to the Western world. Most of those laws pertaining to such crimes as murder, stealing, and rape are maintained by a majority consensus. However, as times change and specific laws regarding human behavior are revised, the relationship between private morality and public policy raises many new questions.

Central to the debate is the fundamental question of how far one may legitimately go within a democratic society to impose his moral beliefs and standards on others. Since virtually everyone believes murder is morally wrong, no one is claiming that prohibitions against murder represent the imposition of religion on public morality. But in a very real way, that is exactly what it is! We must understand that all legislated morality is the imposition of someone's moral belief system.

When does private morality become a problem in relation to public policy? The answer is when those private beliefs are not shared by the common majority. For example, many evangelical Christians believe that smoking cigarettes and drinking alcohol are wrong because they defile the body, which is the temple of God. Suppose that a group of Christians with such beliefs were to gain political control in America and outlaw alcohol and cigarettes. Other Christians who are not opposed to smoking or drinking would claim that their individual rights to personal freedom were being denied. The end result would be a replay of Prohibition.

This is an issue which most evangelicals have not clearly considered. There is a far greater justification to oppose abortion as the murder of the unborn than there is to outlaw smoking in public places. The fundamental violation of the rights of the unborn and the resultant slaughter of the innocents must elicit a greater moral outrage than the question of mixed swimming as a permissible activity. We must choose carefully the moral standards we seek to make public policy.

It is unfortunate that so many conservative leaders have failed to understand this distinction. For example, what an evangelist believes about whether the Jews can get their prayers answered may go over fine in a Southern Baptist Church in Oklahoma or Texas, but it doesn't play well at all on public television in New York City!

Here is where we must rethink the application of our personal beliefs to the development of public policy. The standard of morality within the evangelical community is based upon our commitment to propositional revelation derived from what we believe to be inerrant biblical truth. We believe the Bible is God's inspired revelation to society. We accept its propositional statements as authoritative guidelines for personal and social behavior. Therefore, to us, Christianity is a way of life, not a collection of traditional rituals. In contrast to the liberal mainline churches that have supported the secularizing of public institutions, we have encouraged the free expression of religion in society.

But we must be honest with ourselves and admit that we generally assume that the public expression of religion will be Christian. What would we say if it were Jewish, Mormon, Adventist, Jehovah's Witness, or New Age spiritism? The average fundamentalist or evangelical would charge that public institutions were being used to promote false or alien religions. Thus we need to realize that true religious freedom provided by the First Amendment applies to all religions, not just our own.

The evangelical-fundamentalist movement is not without extremists, but it is unfair to judge the entire movement by the radical statements of a few. We must reject hit lists, name-calling, manipulation, and other coercive attempts to hijack the political process. We stand opposed to those who make imprecatory prayers, bomb abortion clinics, and call opponents "satanic devils." Just as the

Jewish community does not wish to be judged by the bigotry of Rabbi Meir Kahane, who advocates the deportation of all Arabs from Israel, neither do we wish to be judged by the extremist pronouncements of the fundamentalist and evangelical fringe.

Our faith is deeply rooted in our commitment to the inspired Word of God. A position on public policy that extends to others the rights we wish to enjoy ourselves does not in any way diminish the strength of our theological convictions. In the theological domain of our private religion, we seek no change, conciliation, or compromise. When we state that our objective is to evangelize the world, we mean exactly that. When we state that salvation is predicated upon faith in Christ, and not baptism, confession, or church membership, we mean exactly that. These beliefs are not anti-Catholic, anti-Jewish, or anti-Muslim; they are expressions of what we believe. We have always preached the same message and we do not intend to change now for the sake of being accepted by society. To do so would be intellectually dishonest and a tragic denial of our religious heritage.[47]

The ultimate mission of the Church is above political parties and personalities. Thus, the Church must never become so entangled in the political process that it cannot objectively criticize and confront it. But neither can the Church exist in a hermetically sealed environment where it is conveniently divorced from the political process by a self-imposed monasticism.

We believe the First Amendment prohibits the establishment of a state religion and thereby protects the rights of all religions. At the same time, it does not advocate the exorcism of God and religion from society. Therefore, religion must neither dominate the political process nor be dominated by it. We must always be free to worship God according to the dictates of our consciences, and we must also be free to exercise our political rights and responsibilities as good citizens. While we are concerned about the erosion of our traditional Judeo-Christian values, we dare not assume that America's moral woes can be corrected simply by legislative action.

We must remain committed to an America that is pluralistic in the broadest sense. We must be willing to protect the rights of all minorities whether they share our faith or not. That means we must defend the rights of Mormons to send their missionaries knocking on our doors, so we can equally defend our own liberty to knock on their doors.

We must seek to influence the political process in the highest tradition of American politics. We must reject the use of manipulative power politics and inhumane methods to accomplish our goals. While we may verbally battle with others in the process, we must live with them in peace as fellow Americans.

2. Democracy versus Theocracy. In any discussion of the influence of Christian values on public policy, one must consider the contrast between democracy and theocracy. Ironically, many of those who have always extolled the virtue of American democracy are now advocating a Christian theocracy.[48] Unfortunately, the two political entities are mutually exclusive. *Theocracy* means the rule of God, whereas democracy means the rule of the people.

The concept of a theocracy is rooted in the Old Testament community of Israel. God was declared to be the head of state and His law was the legal structure of society. Even after Israel had judges and kings as rulers, they were considered intermediaries between God and the people. The success of their reigns was judged by their fidelity to the law. However, with the collapse of the kingdoms of Israel and Judah, the Jews found themselves dominated by foreign powers. By the time of Christ, the anticipation of a political messiah who would expel the Romans was sky high. When Jesus refused to become a king in this manner, many turned away in disbelief.

Jesus flatly announced, ''My kingdom is not of this world . . .'' (John 18:36). Otherwise, He explained, His servants would fight to defend it and Him. But since His was the Kingdom of God (or heaven), it could defend itself. For this reason, Christians have historically viewed themselves as citizens of two kingdoms: one earthly and the other heavenly. Saint Augustine explained this dual citizenship as belonging to both the city of man and the city of God.[49]

There has always been a great deal of discussion as to how the Christian ought to relate to the earthly kingdom. In examining the basic models for the relationship of the Church to the world, Robert Webber suggests three classical Reformation models:[50]

1. *Anabaptist: Antithesis.* The Anabaptist view emphasized that the believer's obligation was to live by the standards of the Kingdom of God in separation from the evils of this world as a spiritual community or brotherhood.
2. *Lutheran: Paradox.* The Lutheran view acknowledges the fact that the believer is a citizen of two kingdoms (earthly and heavenly) and that he has obligations of citizenship to both. Therefore, he lives in tension between both domains.
3. *Calvinist: Transformation.* The Calvinistic view holds that it is the task of the Church to transform society so that the Church may bring order out of chaos in the world. According to this view, God is sovereign over both realms and He extends His rule through the influence of His Church in society.

We still see all three models operating in some form today. The pietists, Baptists, and Mennonites have generally stayed out of politics and public policy debates. Lutherans have tended to favor democracy and its freedom of religion as an appropriate structure to hold the opposing forces of politics in check. Calvinists have either gone to the extreme of neglecting society because of their confidence in God's sovereignty or they have tried to reconstruct it altogether. These are, of course, simplified views of a very complex issue.

Rather than pit these three models against one another, Webber calls for a "new theological consensus" which recognizes the following:[51]

1. The orders of creation are under God.
2. Evil powers work through existing structures.
3. Christ is victorious over these evil powers.
4. The Church is Christ's witness to evil.
5. The Church lives in eschatological hope of Christ's return.

It seems apparent that there are elements of truth in each of these models. The Church has been given both a spiritual and social mandate in this world. We are to maintain our spiritual vitality by coming apart from the world and living uniquely unto God. But we must, at the same time, continue to live within the tension of our current moment in history. While our ultimate goal is the transformation of society by the power of the Gospel, we must cling to democracy as the best form of freedom available to fallen man today. In the context of democratic freedom, we can and should work to see the principles of God exonerated in our society.

Therefore, while the ideals and goals of today's Christian "reconstructionists" may be admirable, their theocratic approach makes them, in Clark Pinnock's words, "the liberation theologians of the Right."[52] As theonomists, they advocate the imposition of God's law on society by force if necessary.[53] As post-millennialists, they believe that the Church and the Kingdom are synonymous and that it is the duty of the Church to bring in the Kingdom on earth.[54] As reconstructionists, they advocate the total reconstruction of society: education, religion, law, and the economy rebuilt along the lines of a Christian theocracy.[55]

Because the modern advocates of theocracy have written prolifically, they have made a great contribution to refining the religion and politics debate. Their material reflects a serious appreciation for biblical truth and its application to society. They have proposed a carefully considered agenda. Unlike many of the New Right, they have proposed a logically consistent system of thought that has application to virtually every area of public policy.

The proponents of a theocratic reconstruction of society are to be commended for their serious scholarship and well-reasoned argumentation. However, it is also these qualities that make the reconstructionists so appealing to political neophytes. They seem to be providing the extremists in the New Right with a clearly defined agenda that is antihumanist, antisecularist, and antisocialist. As a result, some of the most contradictory allies imaginable have rallied to this cause, including fundamentalists, charismatics, and even some groups with cultic overtones.[56] It would be most helpful if both reconstructionists and nonreconstructionist conservatives could refine their argumentation to hammer out a more consistent position.

The major premise of the reconstructionists is that of a postmillennial eschatology. Believing that the Church is the expression of God's Kingdom on earth, they anticipate a victorious triumph of the Church over the forces of evil *prior* to the return of Christ. They believe the Lord will return *after* the Millennium to judge the world.

Following the basic beliefs of dominion theology, reconstructionists advocate the imposition of Old Testament law on all of society. Thus, in a reconstructed society, unbelievers will not be tolerated, the unrepentant will be executed, and lawbreakers will pay dearly for their crimes.

Richard Neuhaus has observed of reconstructionists that "their importance lies not in their interpretation of the biblical text, but in their reinforcement of a political philosophy that is profoundly hostile to democratic pluralism." Accordingly, democracy is viewed as a "heresy" and is to be tolerated only until the righteous can seize power and turn the public square into the temple of God.[57]

This is precisely where the debate must be resolved between democracy and theocracy. Even premillennialists will agree that democracy is the second-best option to a true theocracy with Christ ruling in person on the earth. However, premillennialists believe this will never happen during the Church Age and will only occur *after* the return of Christ to earth. Therefore, premillennialists and amillennialists have generally preferred democracy as the best possible human form of government this side of Christ's return.

There can be no doubt that the Church in America has flourished in a democracy where free choice is permitted and encouraged. To advocate the elimination of the system by which we have been so blessed seems dangerous and foolish. One need only look at the disastrous attempts at humanly established theocracies throughout Church history to see the problems inherent in such a system. Attempts at Geneva, though exemplary at first, faded into oblivion. The theocracy at Muenster, Germany, was a disaster, and Luther openly opposed it. Even the English Puritan revolution and the reconstruction of Parliament under Cromwell crumbled from internal conflict among the saints. Tired of their oppressive rules, the English people opted for the restoration of monarchy and the Puritans were ejected.[58]

Nevertheless, the evangelical movement today is far from resolving this problem. Too many questions remain unanswered. If we are going to oppose unjust laws such as abortion on demand, how far do we go to prevent murder? If we believe it is right to impose morality to prevent injustice, how far do we go? Where do we draw the line between morality and freedom? If the reconstructionists were to eliminate democracy, who is to say that some more sinister and totalitarian form of government would not replace it and use their laws and structures to outlaw Christianity?

Whatever conclusions we reach regarding the relationship of biblically based standards of morality to public policy, it does not seem wise even to think about eliminating democracy when it is the one great hope of freedom in a sin-cursed world. As one theologian put it: "Democracy is possible because of man's capacity for justice and necessary because of man's inclination to injustice."[59]

3. Cobelligerency versus Extremism. It has often been stated that politics involves the art of compromise. This is especially true in a democratic society where everything is decided by vote. Political alliances are often formed among voting blocs of power or influence (such as labor, education, white, black, Hispanic, northern, southern, western, Jewish, Catholic, Protestant, and now, evangelical). In many cases, absolutists and idealists within these blocs are asked to sacrifice their ultimate goals for more realistic ones. Sometimes it is necessary for groups opposing each other on some issues to unite their efforts on others.

When Christians become seriously involved in politics, they are thrust into the arena of compromise, negotiation, and concession. For example, evangelicals were generally wary of George Bush in 1980. But Reagan's campaign strategists felt they needed him to balance the Republican ticket. Despite objections, evangelicals who wanted Reagan in the White House had to concede to Bush as the vice-president. Later, Reagan's success and acceptance by evangelical conservatives was generally accorded to Bush as well.[60]

When the Moral Majority was formed in 1979, it was faced with the issue of cobelligerency almost immediately. They found ready support for some of their positions on abortion, homosexuality, pornography, and the Equal Rights Amendment (ERA) from Catholics, Jews, and Mormons. Yet some fundamentalists were uncomfortable cooperating even with other fundamentalists of a slightly different stripe and chose to stand alone or form their own alliances.[61]

Two basic questions arise over this issue: (1) Do we actually dilute our position by cooperating politically with those outside our theological circles? (2) Can we ever make a significant difference alone? We believe the answer to the first question is not necessarily, and the answer to the latter is not likely.

Certainly cobelligerent allies such as pro-life Catholics and evangelicals have great differences theologically as well as politically. They may agree on their opposition to abortion, but disagree on the issue of nuclear defense or homosexual rights. However, it should be clear by now that the extremist position, no matter how ideologically satisfying, has not stopped the slaughter of the unborn. Cobelligerent alliances have worked in the past to halt ERA and the so-called gay rights movement, and it stands to reason that they could work again as needed.

Without alliances between fundamentalist-evangelical Christians and those of other faiths (at times even those of no particular faith), we cannot realistically hope to see significant political change. Cal Thomas has argued that on some issues, we may find it necessary to accomplish part of our agenda as opposed to none of it.[62] For example, he argues that many antiabortionists took such an idealistically severe position on no abortions for any reason that more moderate, proposed legislation failed.

Carl F. H. Henry has astutely observed that two things in a pluralistic society remain for evangelicals to clarify: (1) How do we develop moral values into legislation? (2) How do we appropriately address our concerns to a civil government that is committed to preventing religion from dominating the state?[63]

In the meantime Henry argues that "secular society is beginning to run away from us and we must overtake it. While purists have been asking how to seal off the Church from the world, the world seems increasingly bent on sealing itself off from us." He argues further that "raw naturalists" and "radical humanists" do not outnumber us, but they often "outmaneuver and outwit us."

Richard Mouw raises the equally challenging observation that our society is not just one culture, but a complexity of many cultures.[64]

Therefore, the pure Gospel of Jesus Christ must stand above the culture, calling all cultures to Him, while still speaking effectively to those within each culture.

It is for these reasons that we believe cooperation in the form of cobelligerency is a more effective policy than idealistic extremism. While each community of believers ought to hold to its ideals, we may find it necessary to form political alliances with those who differ with us on other issues. If a fire were to break out and we began throwing buckets of water on it and someone came along to help us put out the fire, we would not ask him to enumerate all his personal beliefs. We would most likely accept his help until the fire was out.

We are committed to principles, not political parties. We are committed to protecting the life of the unborn and defending the nation of Israel. We are concerned about the growing industries of pornography and illegal drugs, and the increasing role of government in religious affairs. We are proponents of a strong defense as the best deterrent to nuclear war, and from that position of strength negotiating the verifiable elimination of nuclear weapons. When political platforms converge with our agenda, we support them. When they do not, we oppose them. We advocate cobelligerency with others who share our moral, social, and political concerns. We are exercising our American citizenship and doing what other special interest and minority groups have been doing for years.

This is exactly how cobelligerency works. Those who hold the same beliefs on a socio-political issue join forces to effect legislative or judicial change on that issue. This does not mean that an evangelical must become a Mormon or vice versa. Rarely have such alliances caused people to change their religious beliefs. But when such alliances have been formed effectively, significant political change has resulted from their combined influence.

4. Moral Agenda versus Political Pragmatism. There are many issues facing the Church today that have political implications. However, these issues range from social and moral issues to international military concerns. One of the problems with the New Right agenda is that it ends up with a shotgun approach to these problems.

One day the focus is on abortion, the next day it is on communist expansion in Central America, and the next day it is on South Africa.

We believe that while all these issues are important, such a multifaceted approach to evangelical political involvement dilutes our attention from those issues which could be effectively influenced. We need a clear agenda, based upon a list of priorities for evangelical involvement.

Since our initial involvement in politics was provoked by moral concerns, those issues with clearly defined moral implications ought to take precedence over issues of pure political pragmatism. Unfortunately, this has not been the case. The New Right has uncritically accepted the conservative position on a wide variety of subjects, ranging from how to deal with the Sandinistas, the Palestinians, and the Arabs, to the issue of apartheid in South Africa. While we oppose communist expansion in Latin America, support the legitimacy of the state of Israel, detest Iranian-backed terrorism, and oppose the destabilization of South Africa, we also believe that evangelicals in the New Right have not clearly and consistently thought out the best methods of dealing with these problems.

In many cases we have given uncritical support to the administration because we helped elect them. One has to wonder what position conservative evangelicals would have taken toward the INF treaty with Russia if Jimmy Carter had signed it instead of Ronald Reagan!

We believe it is of vital importance that Christians clearly define the moral limits of their political involvement. It is one thing to oppose abortion, pornography, homosexuality, or sex education on the grounds of our religious beliefs. It is another matter altogether to oppose matters of international relations or world economy on the same basis. While we may have very definite opinions and preferences in those regards, we need to clearly distinguish which issues are religiously and morally based and which are purely pragmatic preferences.

5. Long-Range Consistency versus Single-Issue Zealotry.   One of the ironies of our political involvement has been that we have diluted our influence with too wide an agenda while simultaneously getting overly involved in single-issue causes. We can, for example, mobilize thousands for an antiabortion demonstration on January 22 (the anniversary of *Roe* v. *Wade*) and almost forget about the issue during the rest of the year.

Critics of the New Right have often accused us of being too limited and narrow in our focus. We scream about an issue while it is popular within our circles to do so and then quickly forget it when something else comes along. It is unfortunately true that some are unwilling to make the kind of long-range commitments necessary to bring about permanent change. More than one critic has predicted that we will soon tire of all this and give up the struggle. It is in this regard that leaders like Tim and Beverly LaHaye are to be commended for their long-term commitment to conservative political causes through the American Coalition for Traditional Values (ACTV) and Concerned Women for America (CWA).

At the same time, however, we must recognize the right of those like Jerry Falwell to pull back from politics for a while. Others like Pat Robertson may choose to continue their involvement. Evangelicals must recognize that various individuals will differ in their levels of involvement. Their motives for this may differ from one person to the next. Either way, conservative evangelicals as a movement need a long-range strategy for political involvement that is designed to influence American politics in the highest spirit of the democratic tradition. We need a commitment that transcends individual leaders and represents the concerns of the people themselves. We need a long-term commitment that will not allow us to give up on social-moral-political issues simply because our position is not popular or politically expedient.

Christians in the nineteenth century were long-termers. David Livingstone forsook the comforts of home to invest his life in the missionary enterprise in Africa. He was part of a generation of Christians who proved that they cared about the needs of others by investing their lives to help them. Livingstone later remarked that all that he lost was worth it in the light of eternity.[65]

Today's Christians are faced with a great dilemma as we approach the end of the twentieth century and the dawn of a new millennium of Church history. We are confronted with a choice forced upon us by our materialistic and technologically advanced society. We must decide between comfort and commitment. We must decide whether we will pay the price for freedom and justice. We must decide whether we will give all we have for society or take all we can for ourselves. The choice is up to us!

Chapter Eight

A Critical
Self-evaluation
of the New Right

Why do you look at the speck of sawdust in your brother's eye and pay no attention to the plank in your own eye?

Matthew 7:3 (NIV)

 Self-evaluations are a lot like looking into the mirror. At first glance, we see the image of the whole, which may look pretty good or pretty awful. Further inspection reveals the details not apparent with a casual glance. Our purpose in this chapter is to examine the strengths and weaknesses of conservative evangelical political involvement. It is not our intention to be harsh, so much as it is to help us better evaluate ourselves. We write in the spirit of self-criticism, but not self-condemnation.

In a similar evaluation of Christian political thought, Richard J. Mouw, professor of philosophy at Calvin College in Grand Rapids, Michigan, calls for a "painful self-examination, as well as an openness to the accounts of other perspectives."[1] He reminds us that human ills and wrongs are often "rooted in political life" and are sometimes manifestations of "institutionalized sin," such as in the case of totalitarian governments which "deliberately enforce unjust laws and practices."[2] Carl F. H. Henry has also called upon evangelical leaders to speak "self-critically of evangelical ambiguities, hesitancies, and compromises."[3]

137

It is in this spirit that we seek to ask hard questions of ourselves in the hope that we will ultimately be more effective in our social and political endeavors. We believe in the legitimacy of Christian involvement in social and political issues. We believe that the Christian public needs to be knowledgeable and well-informed about the issues which affect the free exercise of religion and human rights in our society.

John Stott has stated that any Christian perspective on human rights must include an affirmation of human dignity and equality. He argues forcibly that Christians must accept responsibility for the rights and freedoms of others and that we must take more seriously our responsibility to set an example to other communities, both religious and secular.[4] To date, our efforts have suffered from poor planning, misguided efforts, naive expectations, and our own self-indulgence.

Despite all our troubles, evangelicals have brought three issues to the fore in the current political debate:

1. Moral Decay in Our Society. While we ourselves have sometimes become the perpetrators of the very evils we decry, we have nevertheless exposed the fact that modern society is coming apart at its moral seams. Sex, drugs, materialism, greed, and power have become symbols of America to the rest of the world.

2. Evangelical Voting Strength. While we may not have enough votes to determine the outcome of every election, we certainly have enough votes to make a significant difference in American politics. No longer can we sit back and do nothing on the pretext that we are too few to make a difference.

3. Growing Tension Between Secularism and Religion. Most evangelicals become politically active to prevent secularism from dominating our society. We are more concerned about holding secularism in check than we are in controlling the political process. But the resulting debate has made it clear that these are ideologies whose agendas are diametrically opposed.

Any serious discussion of religion, politics, and the media must deal with these three factors. One commentator, Martin Marty, has observed that fundamentalists and evangelicals have had too much fun and gained too much attention from their political involvement to turn back now. In evaluating evangelicalism as a social phenomenon with political dimensions, Marty observes that "today's fundamentalist leadership has spotted a power vacuum and has enjoyed beginning to fill it."[5] However, our greatest problems have come within our own ranks. The development and realization of any moral vision with political aspirations can come only as we assess ourselves and our goals honestly.

STRENGTHS OF THE RELIGIOUS RIGHT

There are several positive qualities related to zeal and commitment which characterize the Religious Right. These qualities have energized the conservative evangelical movement at every level and have contributed to its political success.

1. Strong Belief and Values. Conservative evangelical Christians are characterized foremost by their beliefs and values. Whether they call themselves fundamentalists, evangelicals, or charismatics, they all have a strong belief system rooted in their confidence in Scripture. Though they may interpret certain biblical teachings differently, each wing of the conservative Protestant church builds its moral values upon biblical teaching.

It is this dynamic faith in the basic doctrines of Scripture and a personal commitment to Jesus Christ which energizes the evangelical movement. Its beliefs are usually articulated as the "fundamentals" of the Christian faith. These include the inspiration of the Bible, the deity of Christ, His substitutionary atonement, His literal resurrection, and His Second Coming.[6]

These beliefs rest on a confidence in the inspiration and inerrancy of the Bible. The teachings of Scripture on moral issues related to marriage, family, sex, law, order, decency, and basic human rights are viewed as binding on the individual lives of believers. From this flows a strong system of beliefs about adultery, homosexuality, pornography, and a host of other issues.

139

2. Deep Commitment. Because evangelical Christians take the Bible seriously, they also take seriously their personal commitment to Christ and His Church. As a result, evangelicals of all types are generally characterized as deeply committed Christians in contrast to the more nominal Christianity common in mainline religion.

The deep personal commitment of conservative evangelicals has become a driving force in their political involvement. There is nothing reserved or hesitant about their foray into politics. They have plunged into the public arena with the same kind of fervor that characterizes their entire movement. While this may have been disconcerting to the Republican establishment, it certainly left no doubt as to where evangelicals stood on the issues.

3. Genuine Sincerity. Sincerity has also been one of the positive qualities of the New Right. Most of the grass roots members of the movement are sincerely concerned about the moral and spiritual drift in America. These are individuals who truly want to see the basic principles of social decency preserved. They have no political aspirations of their own. They are simply frustrated with government intervention into the soul of the nation and want it left alone.[7] They have nothing to gain by their involvement. In fact, many face scorn and ridicule from those who do not share their concerns.

4. Zealous Enthusiasm. In a time when many people are bored with politics, it is refreshing to see the zeal and enthusiasm which the New Right has brought into the public arena. They have rejuvenated voters who had long been absent from the voting booths because they had given up on politics. They also stirred up an enthusiastic response by their opponents, all of which has brought new life and vitality to American politics.[8]

Like the civil rights activists of the 1960s, these spiritual rights activists of the 1980s have brought a new focus on the spiritual and social needs of our society. Their raw enthusiasm for God and country has sparked a new level of post–World War II patriotism and spiritual revival.

5. High Ideals.   Evangelicals have infused the political process in America with a new transfusion of high ideals. Undaunted by criticism from their secularist counterparts, they have stood firmly upon their ideals of a better society. While there is certainly debate within the evangelical community about how best to implement those ideals, there can be no doubt about the overall value of bringing those ideals into the national debate on public policy.

Evangelical author John Eidsmoe has called for an infusion of the ideals of freedom, integrity, and compassion into our public policies and our international relations. He argues that God has blessed America for upholding these ideals in the past and that He will do so again if we maintain them.[9]

6. Basic Practicality.   Another positive quality of the Religious Right has been its basic practicality in political matters. Conservative evangelicals have shown a great ability to make the political system work for them. Unlike left wing evangelicals who espouse lofty but impractical visions of political involvement or noninvolvement, right wing evangelicals have learned very quickly how to get voters registered, platforms adopted, and candidates into office.

While they have often lacked an appropriate appeal to society's elite, evangelicals have been very effective in communicating to the common man. They have also seen their results-oriented campaigns produce those results very successfully. They were able to block the ratification of the ERA amendment and various gay rights bills. They conducted successful voter registration drives to elect candidates like Jesse Helms, Paula Hawkins, and Jeremiah Denton. And no one can doubt any longer that they helped put Ronald Reagan in the White House twice![10]

7. Popular Appeal.   One of the greatest strengths of conservative evangelicals is their appeal to a populist audience. These are middle Americans who appeal to middle Americans. Their language, ideals, values, and moral beliefs are those of the vast majority of the American public.

Fundamentalists, and conservative evangelicals in general, are usually excellent communicators. They know how to speak to the general public and they are experts at using media and technology. Oddly, as Harvey Cox and others have pointed out, they are good at using the tools of modern culture while opposing its ideologies.[11] Their success in this regard is akin to David using Goliath's own sword to chop off his head!

WEAKNESSES OF THE RELIGIOUS RIGHT

Much ink has already been used to examine the weaknesses of the Religious Right by its critics.[12] However, there has been very little self-evaluation of the movement. Therefore, it is with the sincere hope that our observations may help to correct some of the excesses of the movement that we offer these humble observations.

1. Fanaticism. Highly committed people tend to become uncritically fanatical about their beliefs. Some New Rightists have described themselves as a "charging army" . . . "working to overturn the structures of this country" and building a "Christian republic."[13] This kind of rhetoric from the fringes of the New Right has only provided ammunition to its critics. It has also provoked genuine alarm among nonevangelicals, such as the Jews, who wonder where they fit into this picture.[14]

If we are to be taken seriously by the public, we must consider the implications of our statements. Most conservatives are really calling for religious freedom in America, not a Christian republic. We are not asking for the elimination of Jewish, Catholic, or Mormon beliefs. But we must be more clear about what we are saying.

Nowhere has this been more obvious than in some of the unfounded statements made by Pat Robertson during his candidacy for the Republican presidential nomination. Extremist statements about the "mark of the beast," nuclear missiles in Cuba, Planned Parenthood creating a "master race," and blaming the exposure of Jimmy Swaggart on George Bush were irresponsible remarks that caused Robertson to lose credibility with the general public.[15]

2. Triumphalism. Southern evangelicals have often been accused of triumphalism about matters related to the Christian influence on society.[16] *Triumphalism* is that mentality that overstates one's success or influence. It is the attitude of wanting to announce the score when our team has won and to change the conversation when we have lost.

Triumphalism often causes those in the New Right to claim they are winning even in the face of defeat. It is a kind of optimism gone haywire that prevents us from seeing ourselves as we really are. It is a blind hope that things are better than we ourselves know them to be. While triumphalism makes for great sermonizing, it smacks of a "God-is-on-our-side" prejudice which hurts rather than helps our dialogue with others.

3. Naive Idealism. Evangelicals of all types suffer from a kind of naive idealism that causes them to cling to idealistic concepts which cannot be translated very easily into political action. This is true of left wing, right wing, and even centrist evangelicals.[17] Just because we espouse certain ideals does not mean that they can be effectively legislated through Congress. For example, Pat Robertson implied that he wanted to cut foreign imports in order to encourage American automobile manufacturers, while also eliminating trade unions.[18] Left wing evangelicals like Jim Wallis and Ron Sider have called for the elimination of all nuclear weapons without mutual verification and have even implied that we should eliminate all military expenditures as a gesture of goodwill to the Soviets.[19]

Naive idealism is evident not only in the policies of evangelical leaders, but in the perspective of the evangelical public as well. Many assume that just because a candidate claims to be a born again Christian, he will automatically make a good leader. The people who say this are often the ones who voted for Jimmy Carter in 1976 and then voted against him in 1980!

If we are going to be taken seriously by the major political parties, we must begin asking the tough questions: Is a candidate capable of fulfilling the office to which he or she aspires? What previous political experience does the candidate have? What kind of voting record has he or she displayed in the past? Is the candidate serious about social, moral, and religious issues or just telling us what we want to hear?

4. Uncritical Allegiance.   One of the characteristics of the Religious Right has been an almost-blind loyalty to the Republican Party and an uncritical allegiance to all conservative causes. In order to gain the party's acceptance, some evangelicals have supported candidates whose commitments to moral and social issues were less than desirable. In other cases, their verbal support for these issues was not matched by their personal lives.[20]

We must be willing to back a conservative Democrat who supports the issues in which we believe. We must be willing to criticize wrong actions or policies on the part of Republicans. One wonders how the Religious Right would have responded to the Iran-Contra affair if it had been perpetrated by Democrats! We can't turn a blind eye or a deaf ear when "our guys" goof up and then castigate the opposition when they make a mistake.

One benefit of Christian influence in politics is to raise a high standard for the moral and spiritual evaluation of political issues apart from party loyalties. Certainly Cal Thomas, syndicated writer for the *Los Angeles Times* and a former colleague of ours, has shown that this can be done effectively.[21]

5. Adversarial Confrontation.   Evangelicals are quick to paint their adversaries as the devil himself. Opponents have been labeled everything from "communist sympathizers" to the antichrist! Nobody ever accused us of being afraid of a fight. But despite the name-calling and our willingness to meet the enemy head on, we often lack an effective defense for our own position. We are quick to tell someone what is wrong with their position without offering an effective alternative.

We must be able to do more than just point out political problems. We must offer well-studied and well-stated solutions. If public education needs to be improved, we need to know where and how. If the economy is in need of repair, we must be able to do something constructive about it. This is one of our greatest weaknesses. We can tell you what is wrong with the system, but we haven't figured out how to correct it. We need better communication and input from economic and social advisors to help us develop strategies to make real improvements.

6. Inconsistent Action. We conservatives tend to get all steamed up about an issue, but if it can't be quickly resolved, we drop it. One of our greatest weaknesses is inconsistency. First, we tend to embrace so many unrelated issues (from pornography to the Panama Canal) that we take a "shotgun" approach to dealing with them. It would be much more effective to prioritize our concerns and focus on one or two key issues at a time. Second, we tend to jump from issue to issue based upon whatever is getting public attention at the moment.

We believe this approach confuses the evangelical public and numbs them against serious involvement. The average person cannot maintain a high level of commitment to a variety of issues as wide as abortion, pornography, Contra aid, and the confirmation of a Supreme Court justice. Such a blurring of focus leaves people bewildered.

We must fine-tune our agenda and target our efforts at key issues in light of immediate priorities. For example, if we really believe that abortion on demand is a form of murder, a denial of the fundamental right to life, we must give it higher priority than the issue of aid to the Contras. Once such an agenda is defined, we need to call for an all-out effort in support of it. This strategy has worked well in dealing with ERA, gay rights, and pornography. There is no reason it cannot work again if we will prioritize our objectives.

7. Reactionary Defensiveness. We tend to react defensively to those issues which seem to threaten us personally. However, once our initial response has been made, we tend to isolate ourselves from any involvement in the search for a solution to the problem. Once the gay rights movement was stalled in its bid for minority legal status, most evangelicals ceased any significant ministry to homosexuals. The same is true in a dozen other cases.

If we are going to be used of God to bring about any lasting change in America, we must move from negative reaction to positive action. We ought to be leading the way with innovative new ministries to the poor and needy as well as to those in spiritual need.

AN AGENDA FOR THE FUTURE

We have learned a lot about ourselves in ten years of evangelical political activism. We have learned that real solutions don't come easily. They take serious commitment, long-term involvement, and hard work. It is obvious that we can make a difference if we really want to do so. The choice is up to us.

We have also learned that political involvement is no easy road. It tends to become a drain on one's spiritual ministry. Therefore, some, like Jerry Falwell, may choose to step down for a while or even altogether. Others, like Pat Robertson, may choose to become more involved. The choice must be left up to each individual. Some may feel it is best for preachers to limit their political involvement, allowing Christian laymen to take the lead in those areas.

Whatever shape evangelical political involvement takes in the future, it must include a serious consideration of the following issues:

1. Sharpened Biblical Focus. We need to continue to refine our biblical and theological focus on major political issues to be sure we are on solid biblical ground. For instance, the biblical case against abortion or pornography seems much more substantial than the case for economic boycotts.

We need to be certain that we are using Scripture properly to defend our positions. It is not hermeneutically appropriate, for example, to use verses like, "And whosoever shall offend one of these little ones . . ." (Mark 9:42) or ". . . there was come a man to seek the welfare of the children of Israel" (Nehemiah 2:10) to refer to the problem of abortion.

Much progress has been made in refining the biblical and theological basis of our beliefs, but it needs to be continued and further encouraged. Discussion between theologians and politicians ought to be encouraged as well to enhance better relations and more effective communication.

2. Refined Political Strategy. Our political focus needs to be continually refined to ascertain how we can best influence public policy in the highest tradition of moral suasion in the democratic process. We need to be sure that we are making our presence felt without limiting the freedoms of others.

This balance is always tough to maintain when conflicting ideologies are competing for influence in the public square. While we definitely oppose godless secularism, we are not advocating the removal of all secular voices from society. To the contrary, we are often only trying to prevent them from removing our voice!

We need a clearly defined political strategy for future involvement. Where we can effect legislative change, we need to figure out how, when, and why action should be taken. Where we can mobilize voters to swing an election, we ought to clearly define why we are trying to do so and give ourselves to the task with full commitment.

3. Consistent Involvement.

If we have learned anything at all in these ten years, it is that inconsistent involvement in the political process ultimately accomplishes very little. We need to make it clear that we are here to stay and do not intend to retreat on the issues to which we are committed.

We must also be honest about our objectives. Others will respect us more if we are forthright with them. We cannot, and indeed should not, divorce our spiritual beliefs from our political commitments. Though candidates do this all the time to appear more broadly acceptable, such action is utter hypocrisy. One cannot cease being a Christian simply because he has become politically involved. Such a dichotomy is unfair and unnecessary.

4. Reaffirmation of Freedom.

Critics of the New Right are always blaming us for infringing on their freedoms, when, in reality, they are often infringing on ours. It was the growing threat of secularism's encroachment into national life that provoked our involvement in the first place. While we do everything in our power within the freedoms provided us by a democracy to achieve our political goals, we must also be willing to insure those same freedoms to those with whom we disagree.

Freedom is our most precious national commodity. Millions of people have fled to our shores in pursuit of it, and we must do all that is within our power to protect it. Ultimately, this commitment will affect our policies of public dissent and national defense. America is one of the few countries in the world where one can openly criticize the government or his political adversary without fear of reprisal. This freedom must be maintained at all costs.

5. *Recognition of Human Rights*.   One of our greatest quarrels with the political left concerns their willingness to overlook human rights violations in Soviet Russia while they attack problems in Northern Ireland, South Africa, and Israel. We must be willing to speak out against all violations of human rights without being limited by a political agenda to the left or the right.

The fundamental human rights to life, liberty, and the pursuit of happiness are guaranteed by our Constitution and must be upheld as essential ideals for all mankind. Human dignity and decency are basic to our conception of what life is all about and must be protected by our political and national policies.

With these principles in mind, we believe that our future involvement in the political and social life of our nation can be more effective than ever. We have come a long way from simply wanting to elect a president who was sympathetic to our agenda. We are now in a position to significantly affect public policy in this nation. May God help us to be faithful to Him as we seek to make this a better country to His glory.

Source Notes

CHAPTER 1: THE GOSPEL ACCORDING TO POWER

1. Harvey Cox, *The Seduction of the Spirit* (New York: Simon & Schuster, 1973), p. 16. Cox discusses the use and misuse of the people's religion while tracing his own spiritual journey.

2. Cal Thomas, *The Death of Ethics in America* (Waco: Word Books, 1988). Thomas, now a columnist for the *Los Angeles Times,* has written a powerful and compelling exposé of the weaknesses of the Christian Right.

3. On the Herodians, *see* Bo Reicke, *The New Testament Era* (Philadelphia: Fortress Press, 1968), pp. 104–124; J. W. Meiklejohn, "Herodians," *New Bible Dictionary* (Grand Rapids: Eerdmans, 1962), p. 523; Harold Hoehner, *Herod Antipas* (Cambridge: Cambridge University Press, 1972), pp. 203–213, 331–342. Hoehner gives the most thorough survey on the Herodians as "men of standing and influence whose outlook was friendly to the Herodian rule" (p. 332).

4. On the Sadducees, *see* Bo Reicke, *op. cit.,* pp. 132–156; Joachim Jeremias, *Jerusalem in the Time of Jesus* (Philadelphia: Fortress Press, 1969), pp. 228–232; M. C. Tenney, *New Testament Times* (Grand Rapids: Eerdmans, 1965), pp. 94, 95; A. Gelston, "Sadducees," *NBD,* pp. 1123, 1124.

5. On the Pharisees, *see* H. L. Ellison, "Pharisees," *NBD*, pp. 981, 982; J. D. Pentecost, *The Words and Works of Jesus Christ* (Grand Rapids: Zondervan, 1981), pp. 542–548; Bo Riecke, *op. cit.,* pp. 156–163.

6. On the Essenes, *see* Reicke, *op. cit.,* pp. 168–174; Tenney, *op. cit.,* pp. 95–106; F. F. Bruce, "Essenes," *NBD,* pp. 391, 392.

7. On the Zealots, *see* Reicke, *op. cit.,* pp. 203–249; Jeremias, *op. cit.,* pp. 70–73; F. F. Bruce, *op. cit., NBD,* p. 1354.

8. On Jesus' Messiahship and the concept of a political ruler, *see* Pentecost, *op. cit.*, pp. 236–239; Jacques Ellul, *The Subversion of Christianity* (Grand Rapids: Eerdmans, 1986), pp. 113–136; Hoehner, *op. cit.*, pp. 208–213; and E. F. Harrison, *A Short Life of Christ* (Grand Rapids: Eerdmans, 1968), pp. 150–161.

9. On the history of persecution in relation to the Church, *see* W. H. C. Frend, *The Rise of Christianity* (Philadelphia: Fortress Press, 1984); M. A. Smith, *The Church Under Siege* (Downers Grove, IL: Inter Varsity Press, 1976); Walter Oetting, *The Church of the Catacombs* (St. Louis: Concordia, 1970); F. F. Bruce, *The Spreading Flame* (Grand Rapids: Eerdmans, 1958).

10. Ellul, *op. cit.*, pp. 88, 89, 113–136.

11. Quoted in James M. Burns, *Leadership* (New York: Harper & Row, 1978), p. xi.

12. Charles Colson, *Kingdoms in Conflict* (Grand Rapids: Zondervan, 1987), pp. 265, 266.

13. Adolf Berle, *Power* (New York: Harcourt, Brace & World, 1967), p. 17. This book has been acclaimed as the greatest study on power ever written.

14. *Ibid.*, pp. 37–80.

15. *Ibid.*, p. 37.

16. Colson, *op. cit.*, p. 266ff.

17. John Kotter, *Power in Management* (New York: American Management Association, 1979), pp. 13–23.

18. *Ibid.*, p. 70.

19. Richard Foster, *Money, Sex & Power* (San Francisco: Harper & Row, 1985), p. 179.

20. *Ibid.*, pp. 179, 180.

21. William Martin of Rice University commenting on Jimmy Swaggert in *People* (March 7, 1988), p. 37.

22. Ben Armstrong, "No Superstars in God's Work," *Religious Broadcasting* (April 1988), p. 12.

23. Frank Mankiewicz and Joel Swerdlow, *Remote Control: Television and the Manipulation of American Life* (New York: Ballantine Books, 1978), p. i. This study is one of the most critical and insightful critiques of television from a secular viewpoint.

24. *Ibid.*, p. 7.

25. *Ibid.*, p. 6.

26. *Ibid.*, pp. 5–11.

27. Quoted by Mankiewicz and Swerdlow, *ibid.*, p. 5.

28. E. B. White, *The New Yorker* (1938), quoted by Mankiewicz and Swerdlow, *ibid.*, facing page of Preface.

29. *Ibid.*

30. Cox, *op. cit.*, p. 303.

31. *Ibid.*, p. 305.

32. William Safire, "Fickle Fundies Faltering as a Major Political Force," *New York Times* (March 8, 1988), p. 32.

33. Os Guinness, "God's Gift and the Devil's Gauntlet," *Ministries Today* (March-April 1988), pp. 27–34.

34. Richard Lee, "Don't Blame Ministries for Faults of a Few," *USA Today* (March 1, 1988), p. 10 A.

35. Charles Swindoll, *The Quest for Character* (Portland: Multnomah Press, 1987).

36. Os Guinness, *op. cit.*, p. 29.

37. John M. Montgomery, *Money, Power, Greed* (Ventura, CA: Regal Books, 1987).

38. Personal conversation with the authors.

39. *See* chap. 3, "The New Right Emerges." *See also* Richard J. Neuhaus and Michael Cromartie, *Piety and Politics: Evangelicals and Fundamentalists Confront the World* (Washington, DC: Ethics & Public Policy Center, 1987).

40. For a balanced treatment on Christian social and political involvement, *see* John Stott, *Involvement: Being a Responsible Christian in a Non-Christian Society*, 2 vols. (Old Tappan, NJ: Revell, 1984); and R. C. Sproul, *Lifeviews: Understanding the Ideas That Shape Society Today* (Old Tappan, NJ: Revell, 1986).

CHAPTER 2: THE CURRENT TENSION BETWEEN RELIGION AND POLITICS

1. Jeffrey K. Hadden, "Pat Robertson May Rekindle Religious Right," Associated Press news release (February 12, 1988). *See also*

Hadden and A. Shupe, "No Time to Retreat," *Religious Broadcasting* (February 1988), pp. 66–68. Originally a critic of the Religious Right, Hadden now observes that evangelicals have the votes to make the difference in American politics.

2. *Ibid.*, p. 68. Assessing the pre-election quiet that seemed to characterize the Religious Right, Hadden asked, "Why this curiously pessimistic assessment?" He went on to observe, "The answer is not to be found in the restoration of the Democrats to control of the U.S. Senate, nor in the sagging popularity of Ronald Reagan, nor in the 1987 sex and money scandals of televangelism, nor in Jerry Falwell's proclaimed withdrawal from politics, nor in the theological backbiting between fundamentalists and pentecostals, nor in a dozen other facts that could be cited as evidence of the demise of the conservative Christian hopes for a new political agenda." Instead, Hadden suggested that too many evangelicals had come to believe the negative stereotypes offered by their critics.

3. *See* Ed Hindson, "The Mainline Is Becoming the Sideline," *Religious Broadcasting* (February 1988), pp. 22, 23; Richard J. Neuhaus, "The New Mainline of the New Mainline, Maybe," *Religion & Society Report* (December 1987), pp. 1–4; and the definitive study by Wade C. Roof and W. McKinney, *American Mainline Religion: Its Changing Shape and Future* (New Brunswick, NJ: Rutgers University Press, 1987). According to statistics adopted from the *Yearbook of American and Canadian Churches* (1984), mainline denominational membership losses topped five million between 1970–1982, with the United Methodists ($-1,052,186$), United Presbyterians ($-744,772$) and the Episcopal Church ($-491,687$) being the hardest hit.

4. James M. Boice, "Five Basics for Political Involvement," *Eternity* (September 1987), p. 18. Boice is the pastor of the historic Tenth Presbyterian Church in Philadelphia, the president of Evangelical Ministries, and the editor of *Eternity*. He calls for a biblically based political and social agenda that honors the separation of Church and State and seeks to advance its cause by "moral suasion" and not by tactics of coercion.

5. *See* his Preface to *Piety and Politics*. This anthology is a collection of twenty-six articles, essays, and editorials on the Religious Right. It is the finest such treatment to date and includes position statements and evaluations from virtually every perspective of the religion-and-politics debate.

6. This scenario has been well documented in several studies. *See also* Jerry Falwell, Ed Dobson, and Ed Hindson, *The Fundamentalist*

Phenomenon (Garden City, NY: Doubleday, 1981); James D. Hunter, *Evangelicalism: The Coming Generation* (Chicago: University of Chicago Press, 1987); Dean M. Kelley, *Why Conservative Churches Are Growing* (New York: Harper & Row, 1972). Ironically, conservatives have often criticized liberals for dissipating their energies on social and political pursuits, rather than preaching the Gospel. *See also* the insightful study by Harold Lindsell, *The New Paganism: Understanding American Culture and the Role of the Church* (San Francisco: Harper & Row, 1987).

7. *See also* his address to the National Religious Broadcasters convention in Washington, DC, on January 30, 1988. Also quoted from an earlier statement in *Piety and Politics,* p. 80.

8. Jeffrey K. Hadden, Associated Press news release (February 12, 1988).

9. *See dunamis* and *exousia* in the word study under "might" in Colin Brown, ed., *The New International Dictionary of New Testament Theology* (Grand Rapids: Zondervan, 1976), vol. 2, pp. 601–611. *Dunamis* means power, might, strength, or force. In classical Greek it literally means the "ability to achieve," and denotes physical strength, fighting forces, and political power. *Exousia* means unrestricted freedom of action. It refers to legal and political authority based upon moral freedom. The word is always used in classical Greek of people, and not impersonal or natural forces.

10. This is the thesis of Jacques Ellul, *op. cit.* Ellul argues that Jesus' attitude is not just apolitical, but antipolitical. He also argues that politics tends to nullify the revolutionary nature of the Church. Therefore, in a republic it becomes republican, but in a monarchy, it becomes monarchist. "The Church's fault," he writes, "is to be found in the process of justifying political power and action" (p. 126). A similar position is taken by H. M. Kuitert, *Everything Is Politics but Politics Is Not Everything* (Grand Rapids: Eerdmans, 1986).

11. John Stott, *op. cit.,* vol. 1, p. 31. He states, "It is exceedingly strange that any followers of Jesus Christ should ever have needed to ask whether social involvement was their concern, and that controversy should have blown up over the relationship between evangelism and social responsibility . . . [they] have been intimately related to one another throughout the history of the Church" (p. 19).

12. Richard J. Neuhaus, "The Post-Secular Task of the Churches," in C. F. Griffith, ed., *Christianity and Politics* (Washington, DC: Ethics & Public Policy Center, 1981), pp. 1–18. He defines religion as

"the binding beliefs of a people" and thus the "dominant factor in how they order their lives together." In viewing the rise of evangelical political influence, Neuhaus relies on Pareto's "circulation of elites" to explain that whenever an ideological elite fails to fulfill its political or ideological function, it is generally replaced by one that is quite opposite to it (hence, evangelicalism vs. liberalism).

13. This fact has been bemoaned by Paul Weyrich, "The Reagan Revolution That Wasn't," *Policy Review* (Summer 1987), pp. 50–53; and by Cal Thomas, *Death of Ethics, op. cit.* Thomas argues that the moral values which brought so many evangelicals into the political arena remain essentially unchanged.

14. *See also* discussions and notes by James Reichley, "The Evangelical and Fundamentalist Revolt" (pp. 69–95); Nathan Glazer, "Fundamentalism: A Defensive Offensive" (pp. 245–258); Sidney Blumenthal, "The Religious Right and the Republicans" (pp. 269–286); and Grant Wacker, "Searching for Norman Rockwell" (pp. 327–353), in Neuhaus and Cromartie, *Piety and Politics, op. cit.*

15. This is observed and evaluated at length by Dinesh O'Souza, "Out of the Wilderness: The Political Education of the Christian Right," *Policy Review* (Summer 1987), pp. 54–59.

16. An exception has been Tim and Beverly LaHaye, who have maintained a consistent involvement in conservative politics through their organizations, American Coalition for Traditional Values (ACTV) and Concerned Women for America (CWA). Though often criticized, the LaHayes have remained consistent with their principles in an attempt to provide a balanced approach to conservative politics.

17. This issue has been raised by Carl F. H. Henry, "Lost Momentum: Carl F. H. Henry Looks at the Future of the Religious Right," *Christianity Today* (September 4, 1987), pp. 30–32. A similar position was taken by Elwood McQuaid, "What's Left for the Religious Right?" *Moody Monthly* (February 1988), pp. 12–17.

18. Examples were myriad in the editorial pages of the nation's newspapers during March and April, 1987. *See* J. M. Wall, "The Fall of the House of Bakker," *Christian Century* (April 8, 1987), pp. 323, 324; B. Levin, "Hellfire, Brimstone—and a TV Scandal," *Macleans* (April 6, 1987), pp. 42, 43; G. Hackett, "Paging the Wages of Sin," *Newsweek* (March 30, 1987), p. 28; R. N. Ostling, "A Really Bad Day at Fort Mill," *Time* (March 30, 1987), p. 70; R. N. Ostling, "TV's Unholy Row," *Time* (April 6, 1987), pp. 60–64; R. N. Ostling, "Of God and Greed," *Time* (June 8, 1987), pp. 70–72.

19. T. McNichol, "False Profits," *New Republic* (April 13, 1987), pp. 11, 12; "God and Money" (TV Evangelists—Cover Story), *Newsweek* (April 6, 1987), pp. 16–23; T. Mason and S. Ticer, "The Gospel According to the Free Market," *Business Week* (April 6, 1987), pp. 43, 44; T. H. Stahel, "War of the Evangelists: Unfunny Reflections," *America* (April 11, 1987); T. Muck, "The Bakker Tragedy," *Christianity Today* (May 15, 1987), pp. 14, 15; "Pat Robertson: Why He Can't Win," *U.S. News & World Report* (September 28, 1987), p. 16.

20. *See* Jerry Falwell, *Listen America!* (Garden City, NY: Doubleday, 1980) and "An Agenda for the 1980s," *The Fundamentalist Phenomenon*, pp. 186–223. *See also* Tim LaHaye, *The Battle for the Mind* (Old Tappan, NJ: Revell, 1980) and *The Battle for the Family* (Old Tappan, NJ: Revell, 1982).

21. *See* the examples of "blind allegiance" quoted by P. Weyrich, *op. cit.,* pp. 52–53.

22. Carl F. H. Henry, *op. cit.,* pp. 30–32.

23. Address to the National Religious Broadcasters' seminar, "The Religious Factor in the '88 Elections," at Washington, DC, February 2, 1988.

24. Hadden and Shupe, *op. cit.,* pp. 66–68.

25. This is the position of Jacques Ellul, *op. cit.,* and is certainly implied by Charles Colson, *op. cit.*

26. *See* the works of leading reconstructionists: Greg Bahnsen, *By This Standard: The Authority of God's Law Today* (Ft. Worth: Dominion Press, 1981); David Chilton, *Paradise Restored: An Eschatology of Dominion* (Ft. Worth: Dominion Press, 1981); Gary North, *Inherit the Earth* (Ft. Worth: Dominion Press, 1986); R. J. Rushdoony, *Institutes of Biblical Law* (Fairfax, VA: Thoburn Press, 1965). For critiques of this position, *see* R. Clapp, "Democracy as Heresy," *Christianity Today* (February 20, 1987), pp. 17–23; R. J. Neuhaus, "The Theocratic Temptation," *Religion & Society Report* (May 1987), pp. 2, 3.

27. *See* R. J. Sider, "An Evangelical Theology of Liberation," *Piety and Politics*, pp. 143–159; Jim Wallis, *Agenda for a Biblical People* (San Francisco: Harper & Row, 1984); R. E. Webber, *The Church in the World* (Grand Rapids: Zondervan, 1986); S. V. Monsma, *Pursuing Justice in a Sinful World* (Grand Rapids: Eerdmans, 1984). For an opposing view, *see* L. Billingsley, *The Generation That Knew Not Josef* (Portland: Multnomah Press, 1985).

28. Colson, *op. cit.*, "Christians in Politics," pp. 277–292; "Perils of Politics," pp. 303–312. One might also cite the eventually embarrassing relationship of Billy Graham to Richard Nixon. *See* R. V. Pierard, "Billy Graham and the U.S. Presidency," *Journal of Church and State* (Winter, 1980).

29. *See* R. Clapp, "Democracy as Heresy," *op. cit.* He argues that reconstructionists advocate the use of democracy to destroy democracy under the guise of bringing in the Kingdom of Christ on earth. This position has also been uncritically developed by many charismatics. *See* Earl Paulk, *Thrust in the Sickle and Reap* (Atlanta: K-Dimension, 1986); *Ultimate Kingdom* (Atlanta: K-Dimension, 1984); *Held in the Heavens Until . . .* (Atlanta: K-Dimension, 1985).

30. *See* the comments of Martin Marty, "Fundamentalism Reborn," *Saturday Review* (May 1980); "Old Time Religion on the Offensive," *U.S. News and World Report* (April 7, 1980); John Bloom, "The Fundamentalist," *Texas Monthly* (November 1981); D. C. Maguire, *The New Subversives* (New York: Continuum, 1982); Flo Conway and Jim Siegelman, *Holy Terror* (Garden City, NY: Doubleday, 1982).

31. Hunter, *op. cit.*, pp. 116–154. He observes that evangelical Protestants are "monolithically and persistently conservative in their politics" (p. 117). He also argues that they tend to carry their political views to "extreme, if not fanatical, proportions," which usually results in a harsh and intolerant backlash from the general public.

32. *Ibid.*, pp. 117–129.

33. *Ibid.*, p. 126.

34. *Ibid.*, p. 128ff. (*See also* statistical tables.)

35. *See* E. Hindson, "Religion Is Alive and Well in America," *Religious Broadcasting* (November 1987), pp. 18, 19; R. J. Neuhaus, *Unsecular America* (Grand Rapids: Eerdmans, 1986). Extensive charts and statistical tables reveal that Americans are still intensely religious people. Ninety-five percent believe in God, 85 percent pray regularly, 74 percent feel "spiritually fulfilled," 61 percent believe religion is very important in their lives, 56 percent attend religious services monthly, 55 percent read the Bible monthly, and 55 percent watch some religious TV broadcasting.

36. A. Solzhenitsyn, *A World Split Apart* (New York: Harper & Row, 1978), p. 61.

CHAPTER 3: THE NEW RIGHT EMERGES:
READY—FIRE—AIM

1. In addition to thousands of editorials and newspaper articles, several major books have discussed every possible facet of this phenomenon. *See* E. Dobson, E. Hindson, and J. Falwell, *The Fundamentalist Phenomenon, op. cit.;* J. Eidsmoe, *God & Caesar: Biblical Faith and Political Action* (Westchester, IL: Crossway Books, 1984); G. Fackre, *The Religious Right and Christian Faith* (Grand Rapids: Eerdmans, 1982); R. B. Fowler, *A New Engagement: Evangelical Political Thought, 1966–1976* (Grand Rapids: Eerdmans, 1982); C. F. Griffith, ed., *Christianity and Politics* (Washington, DC: Ethics and Public Policy Center, 1981); J. K. Hadden and C. E. Swann, *Prime Time Preachers: The Rising Power of Televangelism* (Reading, MA: Addison-Wesley, 1981); S. S. Hill and D. E. Owen, *The New Religious Political Right* (Nashville: Abingdon, 1982); J. D. Hunter, *American Evangelicalism: Conservative Religion and the Quandary of Modernity* (New Brunswick, NJ: Rutgers University Press, 1983) and *Evangelicalism: The Coming Generation, op. cit.;* E. Jorstad, *The Politics of Moralism: The New Christian Right in American Life* (Minneapolis: Augsburg, 1981); R. Liedman and R. Wuthnow, eds., *The New Christian Right* (New York: Aldine, 1983); G. Marsden, *Fundamentalism and American Culture* (New York: Oxford University Press, 1980); P. Marshall, *Thine Is the Kingdom: A Biblical Perspective on the Nature of Government and Politics Today* (Grand Rapids: Eerdmans, 1984); B. Ramm, *After Fundamentalism: The Future of Evangelical Theology* (San Francisco: Harper & Row, 1983); L. Ribuffo, *The Old Christian Right* (Philadelphia: Temple University Press, 1983); R. E. Webber, *The Moral Majority: Right or Wrong?* (Westchester, IL: Cornerstone Books, 1981) and *The Church in the World, op. cit.;* W. Willoughby, *Does America Need the Moral Majority?* (Plainfield, NJ: Logos Books, 1981); and R. Zwier, *Born Again Politics: The New Christian Right in America* (Downers Grove, IL: Inter Varsity Press, 1982).

2. "Fundomania" may be readily observed in the extremist work of F. Conway and J. Siegelman, *Holy Terror: The Fundamentalist War on America's Freedoms in Religion, Politics and Our Private Lives* (Garden City, NY: Doubleday, 1982). They go to ridiculous lengths to suggest a fundamentalist plot to overthrow the governments of the world and set up an international theocratic state. They try to implicate everyone from Jerry Falwell to Billy Graham. They accused the Navigators and Campus Crusade of mind manipulation because of their emphasis on Bible memorization and even assert that the Wycliffe Bible Translators are a CIA-funded spy organization in Central America!

Unfortunately, *all* the footnotes in this book are unnumbered. For other examples, *see* Martin Marty, "Fundamentalism Reborn," in *Saturday Review* (May 1980). In this article Marty lumps fundamentalism with all religious fanaticism. For a more objective approach see his "Insider's Look at Fundamentalism," *Christian Century* (November 18, 1981) pp. 1195–1197. For another extremist example, *see* D. C. Maguire, *The New Subversives: Anti-Americanism of the Religious Right* (New York: Continuum, 1982).

3. On the impact of the New Right, *see* W. Martin, "The Birth of a Media Myth," *The Atlantic*, 247:6 (June 1981), pp. 7–16; J. Franklin, "The Religious Right: Its Political Clout Overstated," *The Boston Globe* (July 19, 1981), pp. A1, A4. For a more lengthy discussion, *see* the careful analysis and balanced assessments of J. D. Hunter, *Evangelicalism: The Coming Generation,* pp. 3–15 and 116–154, and J. K. Hadden and C. E. Swann, *Prime-Time Preachers,* pp. 159–174. Both of these studies examine sociological research to verify that fundamentalism and televangelism are certainly significant phenomena in American society but hardly ready to conquer that society, let alone the world. Hunter, in particular, raises the issue of whether evangelicals and fundamentalists promoted Ronald Reagan's success or whether his success benefited them.

4. Martin Marty, "Fundamentalism Reborn," *Saturday Review* (May 1980), p. 38. For other contemporary observations, *see* "The Electric Church," *Wall Street Journal* (May 19, 1978); "A Tide of Born-Again Politics," *Newsweek* (September 15, 1980); "Thunder on the Right: An Unholy War Breaks Out Over Politics," *People* (October 13, 1980); "Preachers in Politics," *U.S. News & World Report* (September 15, 1980); "Politics From the Pulpit," *Time* (October 13, 1980); "The Power of the Christian Right," *Family Weekly* (October 26, 1980); and "Jerry Falwell's Marching Christians," *Saturday Evening Post* (December 1980).

5. Quoted on *Bill Moyer's Journal* telecast, September 28, 1980. Also quoted in Jorstad, *op. cit.,* p. 86.

6. Quoted in *New York Times* (October 25, 1980), p. 9; *Evangelical Newsletter* (November 14, 1980), p. 2, and in Jorstad, *op. cit.,* p. 99.

7. John Bloom, "The Fundamentalist," *Texas Monthly* (November 1981), pp. 178–182; 288–304. This is perhaps the most irresponsible article written on the New Right, though it may rank second to *Holy Terror*.

8. For a survey of nonconformist groups throughout Church history, *see* G. Westin, *The Free Church Movement Through the Ages* (Nashville:

Broadman Press, 1958); D. F. Durnbaugh, *The Believer's Church: The History and Character of Radical Protestantism* (New York: Macmillan, 1968); J. L. Garrett, ed., *The Concept of a Believer's Church* (Scottdale, PA: Herald Press, 1969).

9. For the history of nineteenth-century evangelicalism, *see* B. Shelley, *Evangelicalism in America* (Grand Rapids: Eerdmans, 1967) and J. D. Woodbridge, et al., *The Gospel in America: Themes in the Story of America's Evangelicals* (Grand Rapids: Zondervan, 1979); G. Marsden, *Fundamentalism and American Culture;* W. G. McLaughlin, ed., *The American Evangelicals, 1800–1900* (New York: Harper & Row, 1968). On the influence of pietism and revivalism, *see* J. M. Bumsted, ed., *The Great Awakening: The Beginnings of Evangelical Pietism in America* (Waltham, MA: Ginn, 1970); F. E. Stoeffler, *The Rise of Evangelical Pietism* (Leiden: E. J. Brill, 1971); T. L. Smith, *Revivalism and Social Reform* (New York: Harper & Row, 1965); B. Weisberger, *They Gathered at the River: The Story of the Great Revivalists and Their Impact Upon Religion in America* (Boston: Little, Brown, 1958). In their own way, these authors trace the merger of Calvinist and Wesleyan theology in the development of evangelical revivalism in America.

10. *See* the well-documented and highly interesting study by Timothy P. Weber, *Living in the Shadow of the Second Coming: American Premillennialism 1875–1925* (New York: Oxford University Press, 1979). This entire study is exceptionally helpful in recapturing the mentality of premillennialism on the eve of the fundamentalist controversy. *See also* E. Sandeen, *The Roots of Fundamentalism* (Chicago: University of Chicago Press, 1970).

11. On the history and development of fundamentalism in the twentieth century, *see* G. Marsden, *Fundamentalism and American Culture;* E. Dobson, E. Hindson, and J. Falwell, *The Fundamentalist Phenomenon,* and D. O. Beale, *In Pursuit of Purity: American Fundamentalism Since 1850* (Greenville, SC: Unusual Publications, 1986). Despite their differences, each study acknowledges the crucial role that the publication of *The Fundamentals* played in the formulation of American fundamentalism.

12. *See* E. Dobson, E. Hindson, and J. Falwell, *The Fundamentalist Phenomenon,* pp. 1–26. For a detailed source of reprint material on the history and theology of fundamentalism, *see* J. A. Carpenter, ed., *Fundamentalism in American Religion 1880–1950* (New York: Garland Publishing, 1987), 45 reprint volumes. This collection has been prepared under the auspices of the Institute for the Study of American Evangelicals at the Billy Graham Center at Wheaton College in Illinois.

13. J. D. Hunter, *Evangelicalism: The Coming Generation,* pp. 20–31. He refers to sociological surveys taken in Muncie, Indiana, in the 1920s and Gastonia, North Carolina, in the 1930s to verify that fundamentalism, not liberalism, was in step with the prevailing culture of the day. He further claims that significant shifts in evangelical/fundamentalist thought did not begin until the 1970s.

14. *See* the perceptive evaluation by Dean Kelley, *op. cit.* This book has been acknowledged as one of the most important books ever written on the subject of conservative church growth while also chronicling the decline of the major denominations.

15. *See also* E. Hindson, "The Mainline Is Becoming the Sideline," *Religious Broadcasting.* Statistics adopted from *Yearbook of American and Canadian Churches: 1984.* In a perceptive article on the fundamentalist-liberal controversy, E. S. Gaustad has acknowledged that liberal Protestantism will lose its battle with fundamentalism in the long run. *See* his "Did the Fundamentalists Win?" in M. Douglas and S. Tipton, *Religion and America* (Boston: Beacon Press, 1983), pp. 163–178.

16. Quoted in *Time* (September 2, 1985). *See* cover feature, "Thunder on the Right: The Growth of Fundamentalism," and "Jerry Falwell's Crusade," pp. 48–61.

17. Hunter, *Evangelicalism: The Coming Generation,* p. 116. He goes so far as to view it as a "myth, encompassing an interpretation of what America is all about." Therefore, he argues, conservative Protestants see themselves as a part of the myth itself with a destiny to preserve all that is good in America. "In so doing," he adds, "it fosters and protects its own interests as a religious people."

18. His comments were adapted to the article, "Who, Now, Will Shape the Meaning of America?" in *Christianity Today* (March 19, 1982), pp. 16–20. This perceptive article should be consulted by those seeking to understand the relationship of theological liberalism to the "Great Society" politics and the relationship of theological conservatism to Reagan's "New Beginning" politics. For an expanded version, *see* Neuhaus, *The Naked Public Square, op. cit.*

19. "A Tide of Born-Again Politics," *Newsweek* (September 15, 1980), p. 36.

20. *See* J. D. Hunter, *op. cit.,* pp. 116–130. He notes that the current wave of fundamentalist political involvement is actually less fanatical than in the past and that extremists are in the minority.

21. *Ibid.,* p. 128. *See also* L. Ribuffo, *The Old Christian Right: The*

Protestant Far Right from the Great Depression to the Cold War (Philadelphia: Temple University Press, 1983), ch. 5.

22. "Yuppie" is a slang term for "Young Urban Professionals" who are moving up the social and economic ladders because of increased education.

23. *See* the observations of Jorstad, *op. cit.,* pp. 70–72. He notes the 1977 Gallup Polls which showed Americans were becoming increasingly worried about threats to traditional family stability.

24. Falwell has often acknowledged that he had no real awareness of his potential political clout until he criticized Carter in 1976. His criticism triggered a flurry of responses from both Democrats and Republicans. Based on their reaction, Falwell began to develop a stronger political agenda after 1976.

25. *See* the insightful comments of R. F. Lovelace, "Contemplating an Awakening," *The Christian Century* (March 18, 1981), pp. 296–300, and Martin Marty, "Old Time Religion on the Offensive," *U.S. News & World Report* (April 7, 1980). *See also* Jerry Falwell, *Listen America!*

26. *See* Falwell's "Agenda for the Eighties" in Dobson, Hindson, and Falwell, *The Fundamentalist Phenomenon,* pp. 186–223; and "Evangelical Support for the New Right," in R. Zwier, *Born-Again Politics,* pp. 83–95.

27. *See* J. A. Sproule, "The Social Gospel Invades Evangelicalism," *Spire* (Summer 1981), pp. 10, 11 and the *Moral Majority Report* (Spring 1980), much of which was given over to a response to the criticism of Bob Jones, Jr., against Falwell and the formation of the Moral Majority. *See* the reply of C. E. Hall and J. H. Combee, "The Moral Majority: Is It a New Ecumenicalism?" *Foundations* (April–June 1982), pp. 204–211.

28. C. F. H. Henry, *The Uneasy Conscience of Modern Fundamentalism* (Grand Rapids: Eerdmans, 1947), p. 79. Henry was one of the first evangelical theologians to appeal for united evangelical action on political and social issues. *See* his books *The Protestant Dilemma* (Grand Rapids: Eerdmans, 1949); *Evangelical Responsibility in Contemporary Theology* (Grand Rapids: Eerdmans, 1957); *Aspects of Christian Social Ethics* (Grand Rapids: Eerdmans, 1964); *A Plea for Evangelical Demonstration* (Grand Rapids: Baker, 1971); and *Christian Countermoves in a Decadent Culture* (Portland: Multnomah Press, 1986).

29. These included Christian Voice, Christians for Reagan, Christian Action Council, American Life Lobby, Coalition for the First

Amendment, Heritage Foundation, National Christian Action Coalition, Americans for Biblical Morality, Religious Roundtable, and Stop ERA. The general position of these groups was *anti* abortion, communism, ERA, homosexual rights, pornography, government control of religious schools. They were *pro* morality, family, traditional values, and prayer in schools. All these segments were later recognized by the general public as "Moral Majority" because of the leadership and media attention given to Jerry Falwell. Hill and Owen, *op. cit.*, p. 66, have observed, "What Moral Majority did, then, was to galvanize incipient organizations" to achieve their unified goals.

30. Jorstad, *op. cit.*, pp. 82–85, examines this issue in detail, tracing the use of political "report cards" to Christian Voice and the *Conservative Digest* and their adaptation by Robert Billings, one of the early Moral Majority leaders. Controversy over their use and grading system as a "moral index" reached a peak when several Congressmen rated very high by Christian Voice were convicted in the 1980 Abscam Scandal.

31. *See* Jorstad, *op. cit.*, p. 90. *See* Robertson's own statement on "Christians in Politics" in *Pat Robertson's Perspective* (September 1980), p. 4. *See also* his comments on the October 7, 1980, *700 Club* and quoted remarks in *Newsweek* (September 15, 1980), p. 36, and *The Norfolk Ledger-Star* (September 30, 1980), p. 1. Many within the New Right believed he was backing away from the election just in case Reagan lost.

32. *See* D. Dabney, "God's Own Network," *Harper's* (August 1980) and Robertson's address to the Consultation on the Electric Church at New York University, Feb. 6, 7, 1980.

33. *See* Falwell's comments in *The Fundamentalist Phenomenon*, pp. 187, 188, and his extensive comments in *Listen America!* pp. 55–68 and 255–268. He stated, "I am convinced that we need a spiritual and moral revival if America is to survive the twentieth century. The time for action is now; we dare not wait for someone else to take up the banner of righteousness in our generation. We have already waited too long!" Quoted by E. Hindson, "Thunder in the Pulpit: The Socio-Political Involvement of the New Right," *Foundations* (April–June, 1982), pp. 144–152.

34. Hill and Owen, *op. cit.*, p. 66.

35. Jorstad, *op. cit.*, pp. 78, 79, made this observation very early. What the press did at the rally was to totally confuse fundamentalists, evangelicals, and charismatics under the banner of fundamentalism. Later articles on religion and politics mixed pictures of Falwell's fun-

damentalist "I Love America" rallies with photos of hand-waving charismatics taken at the "Washington for Jesus" rally. A perfect example of this is "Politics from the Pulpit," *Time* (October 13, 1980), pp. 28, 35. This confusion remained in the media until the distinction between fundamentalists and charismatics was given media attention during Falwell's controversial takeover of the charismatic *PTL Club*.

36. Jorstad, *op. cit.*, p. 79.

37. Quoted in *Christianity Today* (September 19, 1980), p. 1071; *Human Events* (September 11, 1980), p. 12; *Christian Century* (September 24, 1980), p. 872. Jorstad, *op. cit.*, pp. 93–95, is absolutely correct in observing that this was the climax of the campaign. From that point onward, the conservative Protestant vote was Reagan's. What happened on November 5, 1980, in the actual election had already been sealed that summer in Dallas.

38. Quoted by Jorstad, *op. cit.*, pp. 100, 101.

39. Quoted by *New York Times* (November 8, 1980), p. 12.

40. *See* details in Hunter, *op. cit.*, p. 125.

41. Hunter, *Evangelicalism: The Coming Generation*, p. 127.

42. F. Conway and J. Siegelman, *op. cit.* Conway and Siegelman refused to debate Falwell publicly on the *Phil Donahue Show* and walked off the set of the *Schulman File* in Toronto, Canada, on February 10, 1983, rather than debate (then) Falwell associates Ed Dobson and Ed Hindson.

43. Richard J. Neuhaus, *The Naked Public Square* (Grand Rapids: Eerdmans, 1984). Neuhaus, a mainline Lutheran, is also a political conservative who advocates the need to restore the role of Judeo-Christian religion to define American public life and policy. He argues that America was neither founded by nor can be sustained by secularism. In a subsequent volume, *Unsecular America, op. cit.*, he argues for just that while defending the democratic rights of true pluralism. *See* his essay, "From Providence to Privacy: Religion and the Redefinition of America," pp. 52–66.

44. *The Complete Works of Francis A. Schaeffer* (Westchester, IL: Crossway Books, 1982), Vol. 5, pp. 413–501.

45. Jon Johnston, *Will Evangelicalism Survive Its Own Popularity?* (Grand Rapids: Zondervan, 1980). He warned against the problems of faddism, celebrityism, technologism, and materialism within evangelicalism.

46. In 1986 he began publicly acknowledging that he would run for the presidency if he got the support of one million people by the fall of 1987.

47. *See* the impressive research of Dinesh D'Souza, "The New Liberal Censorship," *Policy Review* (Fall 1986), pp. 8–15. He chronicles the liberal bias against the Bible and religion in contemporary media.

48. This is in complete contrast to the "other-worldly" approach of so-called evangelical "centrists." In evaluating R. Webber's *The Moral Majority: Right or Wrong?* the review journal *Choice* said it "yields high-sounding principles but no specific program of action. . . . Webber offers only generalities . . . (and) vague implementation" (September 1981), p. 104.

49. Direct mail appeals from New Right organizations often emphasize themes of threatening nuclear war, the possibility of an immediate communist takeover, communist infiltration of society, decadent morals, declining educational values, and, of course, insufficient funds to combat all of this. One group has gone so far as to imply that postal zip codes are a communist plot!

50. Francis A. Schaeffer, *The Great Evangelical Disaster* (Westchester, IL: Crossway Books, 1984), p. 39. He argues that a "Christian consensus" played a significant role in the American Revolution, as opposed to the French and Russian Revolutions. He further observes that the consensus is being lost in society today.

51. The Puritans were especially guilty of this practice. They began by calling the pope "antichrist" and ended up calling each other the "antichrist."

52. Paul Marshall, *op. cit.,* p. 63.

CHAPTER 4: THE BIBLE AND POLITICS: DO THEY MIX?

1. Virtually all of the literature of the New Right carries this theme. This is especially evident in direct mail pieces, booklets, and pamphlets. It may also be seen in Jerry Falwell, *Listen America!;* Jesse Helms, *When Free Men Shall Stand* (Grand Rapids: Zondervan, 1976); R. Viguerie, *The New Right: We're Ready to Lead* (Falls Church, VA: Viguerie Co., 1980).

2. Various themes were developed by leading televangelists Jerry Falwell, James Kennedy, James Robison, Charles Stanley, Pat Robert-

son, Jimmy Swaggart, and Tim LaHaye. Often their backgrounds dictated different emphases in their preaching. Falwell and LaHaye are independents, Robertson and Swaggart are charismatics, Robison and Stanley are Southern Baptists, and Kennedy is a Presbyterian.

3. This theme is developed at length by Paul Marshall, *op. cit.*, pp. 11–19, 66–81; and Tim LaHaye, *The Race for the 21st Century* (Nashville: Thomas Nelson, 1986).

4. This is the major concern argued in Francis Schaeffer's last two books, *A Christian Manifesto* (Westchester, IL: Crossway Books, 1981) and *The Great Evangelical Disaster*. He argues that only those cultures which understand God's Law are capable of true freedom, noting that wherever we have tried to force our system of governance on other cultures "whose philosophy and religion would never have produced it, it has, in almost every case, ended in some form of totalitarianism or authoritarianism" (*The Complete Works of Francis A. Schaeffer*, Vol. 5, p. 430).

5. Schaeffer, *The Great Evangelical Disaster*, p. 141. He argues that accommodation to the world spirit of our age is the most gross form of worldliness possible. For a similar theme *see* D. Hunt and T. A. McMahon, *The Seduction of Christianity* (Eugene, OR: Harvest House, 1985).

6. This is also observed, with a great deal of frustration, by Robert Webber, "The Religious Right," chap. 15 of *The Church in the World*.

7. For a brief history of the founding of the Moral Majority, *see* Dobson, Hindson, and Falwell, *The Fundamentalist Phenomenon*, pp. 188–194. For a wider history of the New Right, *see* Erling Jorstad, *op. cit.*

8. C. F. H. Henry first developed this concept in *The Uneasy Conscience of Modern Fundamentalism*. It is also a major theme in Francis Schaeffer and Everett Koop, *What Ever Happened to the Human Race?* (Old Tappan, NJ: Revell, 1979) and Schaeffer's *A Christian Manifesto*.

9. Most of the literature of the New Right makes little or no reference to Scripture as a guide to their beliefs or practices. In fact, their most frequently quoted verse is 2 Chronicles 7:14, which is used as an appeal for national revival.

10. *See* Jorstad, *op. cit.*, Robert Webber, *The Moral Majority: Right or Wrong?* pp. 23–56; Gabriel Fackre, *op. cit.;* S. S. Hill and D. E. Owen, *op. cit.*, pp. 100–141; Robert Zwier, *op. cit.*, pp. 99–133; R. Linder and R. Pierard, *Civil Religion and the Presidency* (Grand Rapids: Zondervan, 1987).

11. R. J. Foster, *op. cit.*, pp. 178, 179.

12. These concepts are developed under different headings by Robert Webber in his monumental study, *The Church in the World,* pp. 81–142. Webber traces the changing relation of the Church to society from the apostolic era to modern times. He argues that current strategies have emerged from the Anabaptist, Lutheran, and Calvinist wings of the Protestant Reformation.

13. *See ibid.*, p. 121. In this approach Webber quotes Ulrich Duchrow, ed., *Lutheran Churches—Salt or Mirror of Society* (Geneva: Lutheran World Federation, 1977), as interpreting Luther seeing man as a co-operator both with God and with society. This theme is also evident in the Lutheran theologian Karl Hertz, ed., *Two Kingdoms and the World* (Minneapolis: Augsburg, 1976).

14. John Calvin, *Institutes of the Christian Religion,* ed. J. T. McNeill (Philadelphia: Westminster Press, 1960), 4:20.2; *see also* William Mueller, *Church and State in Luther and Calvin* (Nashville: Broadman, 1954), and Richard J. Mouw, *When the Kings Come Marching In* (Grand Rapids: Eerdmans, 1983), for similar observations and adaptations of Calvin's political model. On the worldwide influence of Calvin's thinking, *see* W. S. Reid, ed., *John Calvin: His Influence in the Western World* (Grand Rapids: Zondervan, 1982), especially chap. 1, R. D. Knudsen, "Calvinism as a Cultural Force," pp. 13–32.

15. *See* R. D. Culver, *Toward a Biblical View of Civil Government* (Chicago: Moody Press, 1974), for an extensive list and discussion of various biblical texts regarding this theme.

16. Francis A. Schaeffer, *The Great Evangelical Disaster,* p. 184. He notes that the French and Russian Revolutions produced quite different results than did the American Revolution because the Christian consensus was so much greater in America.

17. *Ibid.*, p. 23. This warning needs to be heeded by secularists in the New Right who are seeking only political solutions to the problems of mankind.

18. R. C. Sproul, *Lifeviews,* p. 206. This volume is a very readable treatise on the secular philosophies which have shaped modern society with appropriate Christian responses. Chap. 13, "The Christian and Government," pp. 197–210, is especially helpful.

19. *See* John 8:44; 2 Thessalonians 2:3–12; 1 John 2:18; 4:3; 1 Timothy 1:9; 4:1, 2; Revelation 13:14, 19:20; 20:2, 3, 10.

20. Sproul, *op. cit.*, p. 207. He is not advocating tyranny, but he is most certainly denouncing anarchy.

21. The simplistic view of total obedience to human government has been popularized by Bill Gothard's "Institute of Basic Youth Conflicts" seminars. While attempting to combat a spirit of rebellion and lawlessness, Gothard advocates strict adherence to God's "chain of command," allowing little or no deviation, even for wives and children victimized by a tyrannical husband or father.

22. The concept of a hierarchy of Christian ethics has been developed at length by Norman L. Geisler, *Ethics: Alternatives and Issues* (Grand Rapids: Zondervan, 1978) and N. L. Geisler and P. D. Feinberg, *Introduction to Philosophy* (Grand Rapids: Baker, 1980), pp. 14–26, 373–427.

23. Sproul, *op. cit.*, p. 209. He further states, "I see no reason why a Christian should not or could not run for state office and serve Christ by being a godly ruler. . . . It may be difficult, but it is still possible."

24. Paul Marshall, *op. cit.*, p. 48. This excellent source should be consulted by all who are seeking a better understanding of the relationship of religion and politics.

25. Following a postmillennial eschatology, they argue that Christians must take over society and transform it by force of law into a Christian society. Leading proponents of Dominion Theology are R. J. Rushdoony, *Institutes of Biblical Law, Thy Kingdom Come, Foundations of Social Order, God's Plan for Victory,* all published by Chalcedon Publications, Fairfax, VA; Gary North, editor of the *Biblical Blueprint Series,* published by Dominion Press, Ft. Worth, TX. These include texts on the family, finances, economics, politics, and foreign policy.

26. For an extensive critical evaluation of Dominion Theology, the Chalcedon Group, and Christian Reconstruction, *see* R. Clapp, "Democracy as Heresy," in *Christianity Today* (February 20, 1987), pp. 17–23. He also includes sidebars on "The Men and Movements Behind Reconstruction" and "The Armenian Connection."

27. Peter Marshall and David Manuel, *The Light and the Glory* (Old Tappan, NJ: Revell, 1977). *See* a further adaptation in their more recent work, *From Sea to Shining Sea* (Old Tappan, NJ: Revell, 1986).

28. Francis A. Schaeffer, *The Great Evangelical Disaster,* p. 184. Schaeffer's assessment is much more biblically balanced in his view of America's founders.

29. *Ibid.,* pp. 184, 185.

30. *Ibid.*

31. J. Combee and C. E. Hall, *Designed for Destiny* (Wheaton: Tyndale House, 1985), p. 47. While we differ with their viewpoint, we greatly respect the admirable work of these two former colleagues at Liberty University, Lynchburg, VA.

32. For a discussion of this plausibility, *see* Michael Novak, "The Moral-Religious Basis of Democratic Capitalism," in C. F. Griffeth, ed., *Christianity and Politics* (Washington, D.C.: Ethics and Public Policy Center, 1981), pp. 54–61. This is also a regular theme in Francis Schaeffer's works, where he parallels the democratic concept to congregational government as reflected in the Mayflower Compact of the Pilgrims.

33. Francis A. Schaeffer and C. E. Koop, *Whatever Happened to the Human Race?* p. 89. This is one of the most significant books of the late twentieth century because it warns the Church of the trends of secularism on the horizon.

34. Louis Berkof, *Systematic Theology* (Grand Rapids: Eerdmans, 1969), pp. 226, 227. Berkof's position is typical of evangelical Calvinism, and in turn, evangelicalism and fundamentalism in general.

35. For a balanced treatment of the complexities of the South African issue, *see* Richard J. Neuhaus, *Dispensations: The Future of South Africa as South Africans See It* (Grand Rapids: Eerdmans, 1986).

CHAPTER 5: ARMAGEDDON THEOLOGY: PREACHERS, POLITICS, AND THE END OF THE WORLD

1. Hal Lindsey, *The Late Great Planet Earth* (Grand Rapids: Zondervan, 1970). A popular exposition of dispensational-premillennial eschatology. It rose to popularity during the height of the "Jesus Movement" in the 1970s. In it, Lindsey dealt with such topics as the Rapture, the rise of the antichrist, and the coming war with Russia. A more recent update is *The 1980s: Countdown to Armageddon* (New York: Bantam Books, 1980).

2. Comments during Reagan-Mondale Debates in 1984, as commonly reported in the press.

3. *See* E. Dobson and E. Hindson, "Apocalypse Now? What Fundamentalists Believe About the End of the World," in *Policy Review* (Fall 1986), pp. 16–22.

4. This issue is raised by W. S. LaSor, *The Truth About Armaged-*

don (Grand Rapids: Baker, 1982), pp. 135–149. *See* 1 Thessalonians 4:17. For a defense of this position, *see* J. F. Walvoord, *The Rapture Question* (Grand Rapids: Zondervan, 1957).

5. The Reorganized Church of Jesus Christ of Latter Day Saints still holds to the Temple Site in Independence, Missouri, which was forsaken by Brigham Young and his followers who later settled in Salt Lake City, Utah.

6. Thomas Goodwin, *A Glimpse of Syons Glory* (London: 1641). For a discussion of Goodwin's position, *see* Peter Toon, ed., *Puritans, the Millennium and the Future of Israel* (Cambridge: James Clarke, 1970), pp. 64, 65 and Appendix I. *See also* Christopher Hill, *Antichrist in Seventeenth-Century England* (Oxford: Oxford University Press, 1971).

7. *See* details in Tai Liu, *Discord in Zion: The Puritan Divines and the Puritan Revolution 1640–1660* (The Hague: Martinus Nijhoff, 1973), pp. 1–24.

8. *See* E. E. Cairns, *Christianity Through the Centuries* (Grand Rapids: Zondervan, 1981), pp. 301–308.

9. *See* J. W. Davidson, *The Logic of Millennial Thought* (New Haven: Yale University Press, 1977), pp. 280–297.

10. On the history of Miller and the Adventists, *see* G. J. Paxton, *The Shaking of Adventism* (Grand Rapids: Eerdmans, 1962), section on "Seventh-Day Adventists."

11. On the history of Russell and the Jehovah's Witnesses, *see* W. R. Martin, *The Kingdom of the Cults* (Minneapolis: Bethany Fellowship, 1965), pp. 34–110.

12. For a discussion of the views of Herbert and Garner Ted Armstrong, *see* J. Hopkins, *The Armstrong Empire* (Grand Rapids: Eerdmans, 1974).

13. Representatives of postmillennial eschatology include: Loraine Boettner, *The Millennium* (Philadelphia: Presbyterian and Reformed, 1957); J. M. Kik, *An Eschatology of Victory* (Philadelphia: Presbyterian and Reformed, 1971); R. J. Rushdoony, *Thy Kingdom Come;* David Chilton, *Paradise Restored: An Eschatology of Dominion;* Gary North, *Inherit the Earth.*

14. Representatives of amillennial eschatology include: J. E. Adams, *The Time Is at Hand* (Philadelphia: Presbyterian and Reformed, 1970); G. C. Berkouwer, *The Return of Christ* (Grand Rapids: Eerdmans, 1962); P. E. Hughes, *Interpreting Prophecy* (Grand Rapids: Eerdmans,

1976); A. Hoekema, *The Bible and the Future* (Grand Rapids: Eerdmans, 1979).

15. Representatives of premillennial eschatology include: H. A. Hoyt, *The End Times* (Chicago: Moody Press, 1969); A. J. McClain, *The Greatness of the Kingdom* (Chicago: Moody Press, 1959); Rene Pache, *The Return of Jesus Christ* (Chicago: Moody Press, 1955); J. D. Pentecost, *Things to Come* (Grand Rapids: Zondervan, 1958); D. A. Hubbard, *The Second Coming* (Downers Grove, IL: Inter Varsity Press, 1984); Tim LaHaye, *The Beginning of the End* (Wheaton: Tyndale House, 1972); L. J. Wood, *The Bible and Future Events* (Grand Rapids: Zondervan, 1973).

16. *See* Allen Beechick, *The Pre-Tribulation Rapture* (Denver: Accent Books, 1980); Guy Duty, *Escape from the Coming Tribulation* (Minneapolis: Bethany Fellowship, 1975); C. C. Ryrie, *Dispensationalism Today* (Chicago: Moody Press, 1965); J. F. Walvoord, *The Blessed Hope and the Tribulation* (Grand Rapids: Zondervan, 1975); H. L. Willmington, *The King Is Coming* (Wheaton: Tyndale House, 1973).

17. *See* J. O. Buswell, *A Systematic Theology of the Christian Religion* (Grand Rapids: Zondervan, 1962), Vol. 2, pp. 393–450; N. B. Harrison, *The End* (Minneapolis: Harrison, 1941). For a discussion of their views, M. J. Erickson, *Contemporary Options in Eschatology* (Grand Rapids: Baker, 1977), pp. 164–168.

18. *See* J. B. Payne, *The Imminent Appearing of Jesus Christ* (Grand Rapids: Eerdmans, 1962); G. E. Ladd, *The Blessed Hope* (Grand Rapids: Eerdmans, 1956); R. H. Gundry, *The Church and the Tribulation* (Grand Rapids: Zondervan, 1973).

19. While both men lean toward amillennialism, neither has written extensively on the subject of eschatology. Kennedy is Presbyterian and Schuller is Reformed.

20. Wycliffe's work on the Pope was entitled *DePapa* (1379) and is included in H. E. Winn, ed., *Wycliff, Select English Writings* (Oxford: Oxford University Press, 1926), pp. 66–74. He wrote, ''The Pope is Antichrist heere in erth, for he is agens Christ bothe in lif and in lore.''

21. This interpretation was first suggested by Otto of Freising (1111–1158) and Joachim of Fiore (1135–1202) with the dates readjusted by Sebastian Franck (1531) and John Carion (1532). As early as 1520 Luther identified the Pope as the antichrist in *On the Papacy at Rome*. In 1545, one year before his death, Luther published *Against the Papacy at Rome, Founded by the Devil*. Similar works appeared by Robert

Barnes, William Tyndale, John Frith, John Calvin, John Knox, and John Bale. For details *see* K. R. Firth, *The Apocalyptic Tradition in Reformation Britain 1530–1645* (Oxford: Oxford University Press, 1979); Christopher Hill, *Antichrist in Seventeenth-Century England* (Oxford: Oxford University Press, 1971); P. K. Christianson, *Reformers and Babylon: English Apocalyptic Visions from the Reformation to the Eve of the Civil War* (Toronto: University of Toronto Press, 1978).

22. J. Owen, "Righteous Zeal Encouraged by Divine Protection," (Jan. 31, 1649), in *Works of John Owen,* Vol. VIII, p. 128ff. Years later in 1683, the University of Oxford condemned this sermon and ordered it burned. It was based on the text of Jeremiah 15:19, 20; Owen compared Charles to Israel's King Manasseh.

23. This shift is generally credited to the influence of John Henry Alstead (1588–1638), Joseph Mede (1586–1638), and Thomas Goodwin (1600–1680). *See* E. E. Hindson, "The Growth of Apocalyptic Speculation in England 1588–1640," in *The Puritans' Use of Scripture in the Development of an Apocalyptical Hermeneutic* (Pretoria: University of South Africa, 1984), pp. 121–166.

24. *See* Ian Murray, *The Puritan Hope* (London: Banner of Truth, 1971); J. W. Davidson, *The Logic of Millennial Thought: Eighteenth-Century New England* (New Haven: Yale University Press, 1977); N. O. Hatch, *The Sacred Cause of Liberty: Republican Thought and the Millennium in Revolutionary New England* (New Haven: Yale University Press, 1977).

25. R. J. Rushdoony, *Institutes of Biblical Law.* For adaptations of his theory, *see* various issues of *The Journal of Christian Reconstruction.*

26. *See* G. Bahnsen, *op. cit.*

27. *See* Dobson and Hindson, *op. cit.,* p. 20.

28. Quoted by R. C. Clapp, "Democracy as Heresy," in *Christianity Today* (February 20, 1987), pp. 17–24. His insightful criticism of postmillennial reconstructionism is most helpful.

29. R. J. Rushdoony, *By What Standard?*

30. G. North, *Unconditional Surrender* and *Backward Christian Soldiers? An Action Manual for Christian Reconstruction* (Tyler, TX: Institute for Christian Economics, 1984).

31. *See* R. G. Clouse, "Views of the Millennium," in W. A. Elwell, ed., *Evangelical Dictionary of Theology* (Grand Rapids: Baker, 1984), pp. 714–718.

32. *Ibid.*

33. *See* the comments of R. J. Mouw, *Political Evangelicalism* (Grand Rapids: Eerdmans, 1973) and *Politics and the Biblical Drama* (Grand Rapids: Eerdmans, 1976); S. C. Mott, *Biblical Ethics and Social Change* (New York: Oxford University Press, 1982); R. C. Sproul, *Lifeviews,* and the excellent discussion in R. E. Webber, *The Church in the World,* pp. 124–144.

34. J. N. Darby, *Collected Writings,* 34 vols. (Plymouth: Brethren Society). *See* W. A. Hoffecker "Darby, John Nelson," in W. A. Elwell, ed., *Evangelical Dictionary of Theology* (Grand Rapids: Baker, 1984), pp. 292, 293; C. B. Bass, *Backgrounds to Dispensationalism* (Grand Rapids: Eerdmans, 1960) and E. R. Sandeen, *The Roots of Fundamentalism: British and American Millennarianism 1800–1930* (Chicago: University of Chicago Press, 1970).

35. C. I. Scofield, ed., *Scofield Reference Bible* (New York: Oxford University Press, 1909; new ed. 1917; 1967).

36. Tim LaHaye, *The Beginning of the End,* p. 28.

37. This is a major belief of dispensationalism. *See* note 15 for references and sources. *See also* J. Swaggart, *The Bible and Prophecy* (Baton Rouge: Jimmy Swaggart Ministries, 1984).

38. Matthew 24:3–30; Daniel 12:1–3; Mark 13:19; Luke 21:23.

39. Quoted in Dobson and Hindson, *op. cit.,* pp. 21, 22.

40. J. D. Pentecost, *Things to Come,* p. 275.

41. Harry Rimmer, *The Coming War and the Rise of Russia* (Grand Rapids: Eerdmans, 1940) and *The Shadow of Coming Events* (Grand Rapids: Eerdmans, 1946).

42. *See* Isaiah 43:5–7; Jeremiah 12:15; Ezekiel 20:42; Joel 3:1; Amos 9:14, 15; Micah 4:6; Zechariah 10:10; Zephaniah 3:12, 13; Romans 11:26, 27.

43. Hal Lindsey, *op. cit.,* pp. 12ff.

44. See Lindsey's *The Terminal Generation* (Santa Ana, CA: Vision House, 1975). This concept is generally based upon Matthew 24:34.

45. *See* Matthew 24:43.

46. *See* Dobson and Hindson, *op. cit.,* pp. 21, 22.

47. *Ibid.*

48. *Ibid.*

CHAPTER 6: THE RACE FOR THE TWENTY-FIRST CENTURY

1. Paul Johnson, *Modern Times: The World from the Twenties to the Eighties* (San Francisco: Harper & Row, 1983). A perceptive treatment of current trends by the eminent British historian. *See also* his "The Almost Chosen People: Why America Is Different," in Richard Neuhaus, ed., *Unsecular America,* pp. 1–13.

2. *See* the development of this theme in Francis Schaeffer, *How Should We Then Live?* pp. 130–166; and R. C. Sproul, *Lifeviews,* pp. 29–76.

3. This issue is discussed by a variety of evangelical writers. *See* R. C. Sproul, *op. cit.,* pp. 113–127; Charles Colson, *op. cit.,* pp. 205–231; Richard J. Neuhaus, *The Naked Public Square,* pp. 94–143; Carl F. H. Henry, *Christian Countermoves in a Decadent Culture,* pp. 31–46; Francis Schaeffer, *The Great Evangelical Disaster,* pp. 111–146; and Norman Geisler and Paul Feinberg, *op. cit.,* pp. 123, 124, 361–366, 400–408.

4. For a brilliant assessment of this method of thinking and its influence on religion, *see* Harry Blamires, *The Christian Mind* (Ann Arbor, MI: Servant Books, 1978), pp. 3–66; *The Secularist Heresy* (Ann Arbor, MI: Servant Books, 1980).

5. Allan Bloom, *The Closing of the American Mind* (New York: Simon & Schuster, 1987). The underlying theme is that higher education has failed democracy and impoverished the souls of today's students. Bloom probes the relationship between education and philosophy, arguing that American education has been predominantly influenced by German philosophy.

6. *Ibid.,* p. 19.

7. *Ibid.,* pp. 25–43.

8. *Ibid.,* p. 34.

9. *Ibid.,* pp. 62–81.

10. *Ibid.,* p. 82.

11. *Ibid.,* p. 85.

12. Arthur Levine, *When Dreams and Heroes Died: A Portrait of*

Today's College Student (San Francisco: Jossey-Bass Publishers, 1980). In this study sponsored by the Carnegie Foundation for the Advancement of Teaching, Levine observes that today's students are self-centered, individualistic "escapists" who want little responsibility for solving society's problems, but who want society to provide them with the opportunity to fulfill their desires.

13. This point is argued strongly by Francis Schaeffer, *The Great Evangelical Disaster,* pp. 141–151. In fact, Schaeffer insists that the "disaster" among evangelicals is their accommodation to the spirit of the age which will lead to "the removal of the last barrier against the breakdown of our culture."

14. Francis Schaeffer and C. Everett Koop, *Whatever Happened to the Human Race?*

15. Peter Singer, "Sanctity of Life or Quality of Life," *Pediatrics* (July 1983), pp. 128, 129.

16. Cal Thomas, "Taking the Hypocritical Oath," in *Occupied Territory,* pp. 22–24.

17. Stuart Briscoe, *Playing by the Rules* (Old Tappan, NJ: Revell, 1986), pp. 98, 99.

18. Quoted by Tim LaHaye, *The Race for the 21st Century* (Thomas Nelson: Nashville, 1986), p. 135. The title for this chapter was taken from LaHaye's insightful look at current trends and future projections for the struggle between religion and secularism.

19. *Ibid.,* pp. 139–142.

20. Sproul, *Lifeviews,* p. 62.

21. Quoted in Sproul, *ibid.,* p. 69.

22. Francis Schaeffer, *A Christian Manifesto.*

23. For a history of this conflict, *see* Ed Dobson, Ed Hindson, and Jerry Falwell, *The Fundamentalist Phenomenon,* pp. 47–77.

24. Francis Schaeffer, *Escape from Reason* (Chicago: Inter Varsity Press, 1968). This concept is discussed throughout Schaeffer's first book and is presented in a limited diagram on p. 43. The concept of the filtration of ideas originating from philosophy and filtering down through the popular culture was one of Schaeffer's major themes in his early writings. Now, more than twenty years later, he has been proven right!

25. *Ibid.,* pp. 43, 44.

26. *See* Richard J. Neuhaus, "Religion: From Privilege to Penalty," *Religion & Society Report* (March 1988), pp. 1, 2; *See also* Norman Geisler, *The Creator in the Courtroom* (Milford, MI: Mott Media, 1982).

27. Colson, *op. cit.,* pp. 220–223.

28. *Ibid.,* p. 221.

29. *Ibid.,* p. 221. He quotes James Wall in the *Christian Century* without a specific reference.

30. *Ibid.,* p. 222.

31. Sproul, *Lifeviews,* p. 35.

32. *See* T. J. Altizer and W. Hamilton, *Radical Theology and the Death of God* (New York: Bobbs-Merrill, 1966); Gabriel Vahanian, *The Death of God* (New York: Braziller, 1961); Harvey Cox, *The Secular City* (New York: Macmillan, 1965). For evangelical responses, *see* John W. Montgomery, *The "Is God Dead?" Controversy* (Grand Rapids: Zondervan, 1966) and Kenneth Hamilton, *God Is Dead: The Anatomy of a Slogan* (Grand Rapids: Eerdmans, 1966).

33. Sproul, *op. cit.,* p. 37.

34. Truman Dollar, "The Drift Away from Life," *Fundamentalist Journal* (March 1988), p. 58.

35. Os Guinness, *The Dust of Death* (Downers Grove, IL: Inter Varsity Press, 1973), p. 17ff. This insightful adaptation of Schaeffer's early thinking represents one of the most thorough evangelical analyses of contemporary culture.

36. *Ibid.,* p. 17.

37. *Ibid.,* p. 25.

38. *Ibid.,* pp. 25, 26, quoting Jean Paul Sartre, *Nausea* (Baltimore: Penguin Books, 1965), p. 191.

39. Guinness, *ibid.,* pp. 28, 29.

40. Zhores Medvedev, *A Question of Madness* (New York: Alfred Knopf, 1971). *See also* "Psychoadaptation, or How to Handle Dissenters," *Time* (September 27, 1971), p. 45.

41. Guinness, *op. cit.,* p. 41.

42. For a general survey of New Age teachings, *see* the Spiritual Counterfeits Project study by Karen Hoyt, *The New Age Rage* (Old

Tappan, NJ: Revell, 1987). On the psychology of cultic conversion, *see* I. Hexham and K. Poewe, *Understanding Cults and New Religions* (Grand Rapids: Eerdmans, 1986). On the influence of Rajneesh and Sai Baba on New Age thinking, *see* Tal Brooke, *Riders of the Cosmic Circuit* (Herts, England: Lion Publishing, 1986).

43. *See* Hoyt, *op. cit.*, pp. 21–32.

44. *See* William Kilpatrick, *The Emperor's New Clothes: The Naked Truth About the New Psychology* (Westchester, IL: Crossway Books, 1985). This is a study of transpersonal psychology by a professor from Boston College. *See also* Garth Wood, *The Myth of Neurosis* (New York: Harper & Row, 1986); and Jay Adams, *The Biblical View of Self-Esteem, Self-Love, Self-Image* (Eugene, OR: Harvest House, 1986).

45. Dave Hunt and T. A. McMahon, *op. cit.*, pp. 77–84. This popular study of New Age mixtures of shamanism and scientism points to the dangers of evangelical capitulation to nonbiblical thinking and its implications for the Church today.

46. *See* Teilhard de Chardin, *The Future of Man* (New York: Harper & Row, 1964); *Man's Place in Nature* (London: Collins, 1966); *The Vision of the Past* (New York: Harper & Row, 1966); *Human Energy* (New York: Harcourt, Brace & Jovanovich, 1962). For an analysis of his teaching *see* N. M. Wildiers, *An Introduction to Teilhard de Chardin* (New York: Harper & Row, 1968); G. D. Jones, *Teilhard de Chardin: An Analysis and Assessment* (Grand Rapids: Eerdmans, 1969); and Doran McCarty, *Teilhard de Chardin* (Waco: Word Books, 1976).

47. Teilhard de Chardin, *Hymn of the Universe* (New York: Harper & Row, 1961). He argued that the convergence of all life is underway, so that material, energy, and psychic forces will eventually combine in what he called an *implosion*.

48. *See* McCarty, *op. cit.*, pp. 83–102.

49. *See* Hunt and McMahon's analysis of scientism, evolution and reincarnation, *op. cit.*, pp. 93–99.

50. *See* D. R. Groothuis, "Politics: Building an International Platform," in Hoyt, *New Age Rage*, pp. 91–106.

51. *See* Art Lindsley, "The Way to a New Life: Transformation or Renewal," in Hoyt, *New Age Rage*, pp. 226–246.

52. Quoted by John Eidsmoe, *op. cit.*, p. 86. Eidsmoe notes the influence of the Puritan doctrine of total depravity on the early American thinkers and their political views.

53. *Ibid.*, pp. 170, 171.

54. John Stott, *Involvement: Social and Sexual Relationships in the Modern World* (Old Tappan, NJ: Revell, 1985), vol. 2, pp. 247–264.

CHAPTER 7: EVANGELICAL ALTERNATIVES: CAN WE REALLY STAY OUT OF POLITICS?

1. This theme can be picked up in Charles Colson, *Kingdoms in Conflict*; D. W. Frank, *Less Than Conquerors* (Grand Rapids: Eerdmans, 1986); Jacques Ellul, *The Subversion of Christianity*; H. M. Kuitert, *Everything Is Politics but Politics Is Not Everything*; Ellwood McQuaid, "What's Left for the Religious Right?" *Moody Monthly* (February 1988), pp. 12–17.

2. Jerry Falwell, "Politics & Religion: Where Is the Balance?" *Religious Broadcasting* (March 1987), pp. 16–29. *See also,* "Falwell Still Fascinated with Politics" (Interview), *News & Daily Advance* (Lynchburg, VA), March 6, 1988, pp. 1, 2.

3. Tim LaHaye (response), in McQuaid, *op. cit.*, p. 17. *See also* his *The Race for the 21st Century* and *Faith of Our Founding Fathers.*

4. For excellent discussions on the nature and definition of politics, see John Stott, *Involvement*, pp. 30–34; and R. C. Sproul, *Lifeviews*, pp. 197–209.

5. This position is argued from a Christian perspective very convincingly by John Eidsmoe, *op. cit.*, pp. 1–24, 54–70.

6. See Ed Dobson, Ed Hindson, and Jerry Falwell, *The Fundamentalist Phenomenon*, pp. 1–26.

7. This thesis is convincingly developed by Richard Neuhaus in *The Naked Public Square*. Neuhaus examines the interrelationship of secular and religious views of reason, morality, and virtue in the debate on religion and public policy.

8. This point has been made very strongly by James M. Boice, "Five Basics for Political Involvement," *Eternity* (September 1987), p. 18. He argues, "In attempting to advance a specific proposal, Christians must depend on moral suasion . . . but they must not retreat from this high position to tactics of mere naked pressure and coercion."

9. Richard Neuhaus, "Christian Monisms Against the Gospel," *Religion & Society Report* (November 1987), pp. 1–3. Neuhaus's remarks are made in a lengthy review of Frank's *Less Than Conquerors, op. cit.*

He astutely criticizes Frank's thesis as a monistic elevation of power-lessness as the solution to the illusion of power. Such an approach, he argues, results in the "abandonment of our responsibility" to care for the world. He also questions Frank's embrace of Marxian class analysis of America as a consumerist, imperialist, capitalist aggressor.

10. Stott, *Involvement,* pp. 34–36. He calls for the development of a fuller doctrine of God and man which recognizes God's concern for the whole of mankind and the whole of human life (pp. 36–51).

11. *See* Stott, *op. cit.,* pp. 19–25, for a detailed discussion of Wesley and Finney's influences on evangelical social concerns in the eighteenth and nineteenth centuries.

12. *See* Stott, *op. cit.,* pp. 77–80; Ed Dobson, "Reflections on the Holocaust," *Fundamentalist Journal* (April 1985), pp. 12, 13. Dobson writes, "We must hear the screams of the children, smell the stench of death, feel the pain of suffering, and never forget!"

13. Quoted in Richard Gutteridge, *Open Thy Mouth for the Dumb: The German Evangelical Church and the Jews 1870–1950* (Oxford: Basil Blackwell, 1976), p. 299.

14. Stott, *op. cit.,* p. 93. He calls for responsible Christian involvement based upon "zeal for God and love for man" that will "seek the renewal of society."

15. William H. Willimon, "The Chains of Religious Freedom," *Christianity Today* (September 18, 1987), pp. 28–30.

16. *Ibid.,* p. 29.

17. Cal Thomas, "The Time is Now," in *Occupied Territory,* pp. 28–30. This excellent book is a collection of seventy-four of Thomas's columns for the *Los Angeles Times.* They represent some of the finest critical thinking on social and political issues available from a conservative perspective.

18. This theme is developed effectively by Tim LaHaye in chap. 1, "Help! We've Been Robbed," and chap. 2, "Who Secularized America?" in *Faith of Our Founding Fathers,* pp. 1–29.

19. Sproul, *Lifeviews,* p. 29.

20. Bush's comments were made at the National Religious Broadcasters' convention in Washington, DC, on January 30, 1988.

21. Paul Johnson, "The Almost Chosen People," in R. Neuhaus, ed., *Unsecular America,* pp. 1–13.

22. This theme is repeated throughout his *The Naked Public Square, op. cit. See also* his "From Providence to Privacy: Religion and the Redefinition of America," in *Unsecular America,* pp. 52–66; "Who, Now, Will Shape the Meaning of America?" *Christianity Today* (March 19, 1982), pp. 16–20; "The Post-Secular Task of Churches," in C. F. Griffith, ed., *Christianity and Politics* (Washington, D.C.: Ethics & Public Policy Center, 1981).

23. Neuhaus, *The Naked Public Square,* p. 30. He adds that the "proper word for the state of affairs in which the political encompasses, or aspires to encompass, everything is totalitarianism."

24. *See* the discussion of the historical background of fundamentalist involvement in politics in Ed Hindson, "Thunder in the Pulpit: The Social-Political Involvement of the New Right," *Foundations* (April 1982), pp. 144–152; Dinesh D'Souza, "Out of the Wilderness: The Political Education of the New Right," *Policy Review* (Summer 1987), pp. 54–59; Richard Neuhaus, "What the Fundamentalists Want," in R. Neuhaus and M. Cromartie, *op. cit.,* pp. 3–18; and A. J. Reichley, "The Evangelical and Fundamentalist Revolt," in Neuhaus and Cromartie, eds., *Piety and Politics,* pp. 69–95.

25. Neuhaus, *The Naked Public Square,* p. 37.

26. *Ibid.,* pp. 216–221. He dated the Great Accommodation from 1890–1920, during liberalism's formative period. Neuhaus follows Robert Handy's observation that this period of the rise of Protestant liberalism became the "second disestablishment" of religion in America (the first having come after the Revolutionary War).

27. *See* Ed Hindson, "The Mainline Is Becoming the Sideline," *Religious Broadcasting* (February 1988), pp. 22, 23; W. Roof and W. McKinney, *American Mainline Religion* (New Brunswick, NJ: Rutgers University Press, 1986).

28. This theme is developed by James D. Hunter in his chapter on "Modernity and the Reconstruction of Tradition," in his *Evangelicalism: The Coming Generation.* This concept is also identified by Stott, *Involvement,* pp. 24–27.

29. Walter Rauschenbusch, *Christianity and the Social Crisis* (New York: Macmillan, 1907), p. xiii. He identified the Kingdom of God with a "reconstruction of society on a Christian basis" (p. 149). This theme is also found in his *A Theology for the Social Gospel* (New York: Macmillan, 1917).

30. For detailed accounts *see* Ed Dobson, Ed Hindson, and Jerry Falwell, *The Fundamentalist Phenomenon,* pp. 47–77; S. G. Cole, *The*

History of Fundamentalism (New York: Smith, 1931); G. W. Dollar, *A History of Fundamentalism in America* (Greenville, SC: Bob Jones University Press, 1973); N. F. Furniss, *The Fundamentalist Controversy* (New Haven: Yale University Press, 1954); Louis Gasper, *The Fundamentalist Movement* (The Hague: Moulton, 1963); E. S. Gaustad, *Dissent in American Religion* (Chicago: University of Chicago Press, 1973); George Marsden, *Fundamentalism and American Culture.*

31. *See* W. R. Hutchison, *American Protestant Thought: The Liberal Era* (New York: Harper & Row, 1968) and *The Modernist Impulse in American Protestantism* (Cambridge, MA: Harvard University Press, 1976).

32. *See* Dobson, Hindson, and Falwell, *The Fundamentalist Phenomenon*, pp. 79–112. New fundamentalist groups were formed from separatist groups which withdrew from the Baptist, Presbyterian, and other denominations. These included the Baptist Bible Fellowship, World Baptist Fellowship, General Association of Regular Baptist Churches, Conservative Baptist Association, Southwide Baptist Fellowship, New Testament Baptists, Independent Fundamental Churches of America, Grace Brethren Churches, Orthodox Presbyterian, Bible Presbyterian, Evangelical and Reformed Presbyterians, and the Presbyterian Churches of America.

33. The history of this era and the early rise of evangelical radio broadcasting is treated extensively by Ben Armstrong, *The Electric Church* (Nashville: Thomas Nelson, 1979).

34. According to the *Yearbook of American and Canadian Churches* (1984), mainline churches lost 5 million members between 1970–1982, with United Methodists (-1 million) and United Presbyterians ($-744,000$) being the biggest losers.

35. Charles Colson, *op. cit.,* p. 304. Colson's perceptive insights need to be heeded by evangelicals aspiring to influence American public life.

36. *See* Dean M. Kelley, *op. cit.,* and E. L. Towns, *America's Fastest Growing Churches* (Nashville: Impact Books, 1972).

37. *See* references under note 30. *Also see* David O. Beale, *op. cit.*

38. *See* Donald G. Bloesch, *The Evangelical Renaissance* (Grand Rapids: Eerdmans, 1973) and *The Future of Evangelical Christianity* (Garden City, NY: Doubleday, 1983); Kenneth Kantzer, ed., *Evangelical Roots* (Nashville: Thomas Nelson, 1978); Bernard Ramm, *The Evangelical Heritage* (Waco: Word Books, 1973); Bruce Shelley, *Evangelicalism in America* (Grand Rapids: Eerdmans, 1967); David

Wells and John Woodbridge, eds., *The Evangelicals* (Grand Rapids: Baker, 1977); John Woodbridge, Mark Noll, and Nathan Hatch, eds., *The Gospel in America: Themes in the Story of America's Evangelicals* (Grand Rapids: Zondervan, 1979).

39. *See* B. A. Weisberger, *They Gathered at the River* (Chicago: Quadrangle Books, 1958); Vinson Synan, *The Holiness-Pentecostal Movement in the United States* (Grand Rapids: Eerdmans, 1971); R. M. Anderson, *Vision of the Disinherited: The Making of American Pentecostalism* (New York: Oxford University Press, 1979); Morton Kelsey, *Encounter with God: A Theology of Christian Experience* (Minneapolis: Bethany Fellowship, 1972); Erling Jorstad, *The Holy Spirit in Today's Church: A Handbook of the New Pentecostalism* (Nashville: Abingdon, 1973).

40. *See* "A Tide of Born-Again Politics," *Newsweek* (September 15, 1980), p. 36; "Thunder on the Right: An Unholy War Breaks Out Over Politics," *People* (October 13, 1980); "Preachers in Politics," *U.S. News & World Report* (September 15, 1980); "Politics From the Pulpit," *Time* (October 13, 1980).

41. *See* McKendree Langley, "Robertson's Run: Going for It?" *Eternity* (September 1987), pp. 11–13; James Kilpatrick, "Born-Again Christians Weren't Born Yesterday," syndicated editorial, *Washington Post* (March 2, 1988). Bakker was out of PTL by the time Robertson's campaign got into full swing, and though Swaggart had endorsed Robertson, he was not actively involved in publicly campaigning for him.

42. *See* Elwood McQuaid, "What's Left for the Religious Right?" *Moody Monthly*, pp. 12–17. This is also implied by Charles Colson, *Kingdoms in Conflict.*

43. Edward Norman, *Christianity and the World Order* (Oxford: Oxford University Press, 1979), p. 32. Quoted by Stott, *Involvement*, p. 33.

44. Paul Weyrich, "The Reagan Revolution That Wasn't," *Policy Review* (Summer 1987), pp. 50–53; Cal Thomas, *The Death of Ethics in America.*

45. Jeffrey Hadden and Anson Shupe, "No Time to Retreat," *Religious Broadcasting*, pp. 66–68; Tim LaHaye, *The Race for the 21st Century*, pp. 76–134.

46. This issue has been raised in the following discussions: Carl F. H. Henry, *The Christian Mindset in a Secular Society* (Portland: Multnomah Press, 1984) and *Christian Countermoves in a Decadent Culture;* John Eidsmoe, *op. cit.;* Stephen Monsma, *op. cit.*; R. Neuhaus and M. Cromartie, eds., *op. cit.*

47. *See* this thought developed by Ed Dobson, "Fundamentalist Fanaticism: Private Religion and Public Policy," *Fundamentalist Journal* (March 1985), pp. 14, 15.

48. While many writers are not clear on this subject, the following seem to be advocating the establishment of a Christian Republic: James Kennedy, *Reconstruction: Biblical Guidelines for a Nation in Peril* (Ft. Lauderdale: Coral Ridge Ministries, n.d.); David Chilton, *op. cit.*; Gary DeMar, *God and Government: The Restoration of the Republic* (Atlanta: American Vision Press, 1986); George Grant, *Changing of the Guard: Biblical Principles for Political Action* (Ft. Worth: Dominion Press, 1987); Gary North, *Liberating Planet Earth* (Ft. Worth: Dominion Press, 1987); Rus Walton, *One Nation Under God* (Nashville: Thomas Nelson, 1987); Peter Waldron, *Rebuilding the Walls: A Biblical Strategy for Restoring America's Greatness* (Nashville: Wolgemuth & Hyatt, 1987).

49. St. Augustine, *The City of God* in W. J. Oates, ed., *Basic Writings of Saint Augustine,* vol. 2 (Grand Rapids: Baker, 1980), pp. 3–666.

50. *See* the helpful and thorough discussion by Robert Webber, *The Church in the World,* pp. 81–144.

51. *Ibid.,* pp. 261–278.

52. Quoted by Richard Neuhaus, "The Theocratic Temptation," *Religion & Society Report* (May 1987), pp. 2, 3.

53. *See* James Jordon, *The Law of the Covenant: An Exposition of Exodus 21–23* (Tyler, TX: Institute for Christian Economics, 1984); Greg Bahnsen, *op. cit.*

54. Rousas J. Rushdoony, *The Institutes of Biblical Law* (Fairfax, VA: Chalcedon Publications, 1983) and *Thy Kingdom Come.*

55. *See* the various works in the *Biblical Blueprint Series* co-published by Dominion Press and Thomas Nelson.

56. *See* Peter Waldron, *Rebuilding the Walls*; Earl Paulk, *Ultimate Kingdom; Held in the Heavens Until . . .* ; R. Clapp, "Democracy as Heresy," *Christianity Today,* pp. 17–23.

57. Richard Neuhaus, "The Theocratic Temptation," *Religion & Society Report* (May 1987), pp. 2, 3. He argues that Reconstructionism "uses the rules of democracy to destroy the rules of democracy."

58. *See* Edward E. Hindson, *The Puritans' Use of Scripture in Developing an Apocalyptical Hermeneutic, op. cit.*

59. Reinhold Niebuhr, quoted by Neuhaus, *op. cit.,* p. 3.

60. Jerry Falwell, for example, endorsed Bush as early as 1983 for the 1988 election.

61. This was true of Bob Jones, Greg Dixon, Jack Hyles and others. On this issue, *see* C. E. Hall and J. H. Combee, "The Moral Majority: Is it a New Ecumenicalism?" *Foundations* (April 1982), pp. 204–211.

62. Cal Thomas, *Occupied Territory,* pp. 28–30

63. Carl F. H. Henry, *Christian Countermoves in a Decadent Culture,* pp. 119–127. Henry contrasts American democracy to the religious totalitarianism of Islam and the antireligious totalitarianism of the communist Soviet Union.

64. Richard Mouw, *When Kings Come Marching In,* pp. 13–60.

65. See Elspeth Huxley, *Livingstone and His African Journeys* (London: Huxley, 1974); Robert Laws, *Reminiscences of Livingstone* (Edinburgh: n.p., 1934); Earle Cairns, *An Endless Line of Splendor* (Wheaton: Tyndale House, 1986), pp. 254–257.

CHAPTER 8: A CRITICAL SELF-EVALUATION OF THE NEW RIGHT

1. Richard Mouw, "Reforming Cultural Calvinism," *Reformed Journal* (March 1981), pp. 15, 16.

2. Richard Mouw, *When Kings Come Marching In,* pp. 30–64.

3. Carl F. H. Henry, *Christian Countermoves in a Decadent Culture,* p. 129.

4. John Stott, *Involvement,* pp. 204, 205.

5. Martin Marty, "Fundamentalism as a Social Phenomenon," in George Marsden, ed., *Evangelicalism and Modern America* (Grand Rapids: Eerdmans, 1984), pp. 56–68.

6. *See* Ed Dobson, *In Search of Unity: An Appeal to Fundamentalists and Evangelicals* (Nashville: Thomas Nelson, 1985), pp. 37–40; Frank Nelson, *Public Schools: An Evangelical Appraisal* (Old Tappan, NJ: Revell, 1987), pp. 13–30; and Ed Dobson, Ed Hindson, and Jerry Falwell, *The Fundamentalist Phenomenon,* 2d ed., pp. 6–11.

7. This is clearly understood by Richard Neuhaus, "What the Fundamentalists Want," and James Reichley," The Evangelical and Fundamentalist Revolt," in Richard Neuhaus and Michael Cromartie, *Piety*

and Politics, pp. 3–18, 69–95. For a personal assessment of fundamentalism by an outsider, *see* Harvey Cox, *Religion in the Secular City* (New York: Simon & Schuster, 1984), pp. 29–82.

8. One need only consult the more than 500 books and articles that have been written on this subject in less than ten years!

9. John Eidsmoe, *God and Caesar,* pp. 212–214.

10. This is now verified by several studies and surveys quoted by James D. Hunter, *Evangelicalism: The Coming Generation*, pp. 116–154, 267–272. These studies revealed that 63 percent of all evangelicals voted Republican in the 1980 presidential election and 80 percent voted for Reagan in 1984 (p. 268).

11. Cox, *op. cit.,* p. 43.

12. *See* Richard Pierard, "The New Religious Right in American Politics," in George Marsden, ed., *op. cit.,* pp. 161–174; Gabriel Fackre, *op. cit.*; S. S. Hill and D. E. Owen, *op. cit.;* Erling Jorstad, *op. cit.;* Robert Zwier, *op. cit.*

13. See examples quoted by Reichly, *op. cit.*, pp. 92–95.

14. This issue was raised at a conference on Jews and Fundamentalism at Indiana University, co-sponsored by the Anti-Defamation League of B'nai B'rith and the Lilly Foundation (January 1985) and at a conference on "Jews in Unsecular America" sponsored by the Center on Religion and Society in New York City (January 1986). Papers from the latter conference will soon be forthcoming as a volume in Eerdmans' *Encounter Series* (1988).

15. *See* the insightful criticism by James Kilpatrick, "Born-again Christians Weren't Born Yesterday" (Syndicated Column), *Washington Post* (March 2, 1988).

16. *See* Martin Marty, "Fundamentalism as a Social Phenomenon," *op. cit.,* pp. 56–68; Nathan Glazer, "Fundamentalism: A Defensive Offensive," in *Piety and Politics,* pp. 245–258; George Marsden, *Fundamentalism and American Culture* and "Fundamentalism and the Southern Baptist Convention," *Review and Expositor* (Winter 1982), 8 articles, pp. 3–145.

17. Stott, *Involvement,* levels this critique. *See* examples of naive proposals in Jim Wallis, *op. cit.;* Ronald Sider, "An Evangelical Theology of Liberation," in *Piety and Politics,* pp. 143–160; J. A. Bernbaum, ed., *Perspectives on Peacemaking* (Ventura, CA: Regal Books, 1984).

18. Speech at National Religious Broadcasters convention in Washington, DC, on January 30, 1988.

19. *See* R. Sider and R. K. Taylor, *Nuclear Holocaust and Christian Hope* (Downers Grove, IL: Inter-Varsity Press, 1982) and J. Wallis, *Agenda for Biblical People* (Grand Rapids: Eerdmans, 1972).

20. This objection is raised by Paul Weyrich, "The Reagan Revolution That Wasn't," *Policy Review* (Summer 1987), pp. 50–53.

21. See Cal Thomas, *Occupied Territory* and *The Death of Ethics in America.*

Bibliography

Armstrong, Ben. *The Electric Church.* Nashville: Thomas Nelson, 1979.

Bahnsen, G., *By This Standard: the Authority of God's Law Today.* Fort Worth: Dominion Press, 1981.

Beale, David O. *In Pursuit of Purity: American Fundamentalism Since 1850.* Greenville, SC: Unusual Publications, 1986.

Bloesch, Donald G. *Crumbling Foundations.* Grand Rapids: Zondervan, 1984. *The Future of Evangelical Christianity.* Garden City, NY: Doubleday, 1983.

Bloom, Alan. *The Closing of the American Mind.* New York: Simon & Schuster, 1986.

Bloom, John. "The Fundamentalist," *Texas Monthly* (November 1981), pp. 18–33.

Blumenthal, Sidney. "The Religious Right and Republicans," *The New Republic* (October 22, 1984), pp. 1–15.

Boice, James M. "Five Basics for Political Involvement," *Eternity* (September 1987), p. 18.

Campolo, Anthony. *The Power Delusion.* Wheaton: Victor Books, 1983.

Carpenter, Joel A., ed. *Fundamentalism in American Religion, 1880–1950,* 45 reprint vols. New York: Garland Publishing, 1987.

Chilton, David. *Paradise Restored: An Eschatology of Dominion.* Ft. Worth: Dominion Press, 1981.

Clapp, R. "Democracy as Heresy," *Christianity Today* (February 20, 1987), pp. 17–23.

Clouse, Robert. "The New Christian Right, America and the Kingdom of God," *Christian Scholars Review* (1983).

Colson, Charles. *Kingdoms in Conflict.* Grand Rapids: Zondervan/ Morrow, 1987.

Combee, Jerry and C. E. Hall, *Designed for Destiny.* Wheaton: Tyndale House, 1985.

Conway, Flo and Jim Siegelman. *Holy Terror: The Fundamentalist War on America's Freedoms.* Garden City, NY: Doubleday, 1982.

Cox, Harvey. *Religion in the Secular City.* New York: Simon & Schuster, 1984.

Crawford, Alan. *Thunder on the Right: The "New Right" and the Politics of Resentment.* New York: Pantheon Books, 1980.

Dobson, Ed. *A Call to Unity: An Appeal to Fundamentalists and Evangelicals.* Nashville: Thomas Nelson, 1985. "Fundamentalist Fanaticism: Private Religion and Public Policy," *Fundamentalist Journal* (March 1985), pp. 14, 15. "Religion and Politics: What About the Future?" *Fundamentalist Journal* (November 1987), p. 12. "A Philosophy of Christian Political Involvement," *Fundamentalist Journal* (December 1987), p. 12.

Dobson, Ed, and Ed Hindson. "Apocalypse Now? What Fundamentalists Believe About the End of the World," *Policy Review* (Fall 1986), pp. 16–22.

Dobson, Ed, Ed Hindson, and Jerry Falwell, *The Fundamentalist Phenomenon.* Garden City, NY: Doubleday, 1981.

D'Souza, Dinesh. *Falwell Before the Millennium.* Chicago: Regnery Gateway, 1984. "Out of the Wilderness: The Political Education of the New Right," *Policy Review,* 41 (Summer 1987), pp. 54–59.

Eidsmoe, John. *God and Caesar: Biblical Faith and Political Action.* Westchester, IL: Crossway Books, 1984. *Christianity and the Constitution.* Grand Rapids: Baker, 1987.

Ellul, Jacques. *The Subversion of Christianity.* Trans. by G. W. Bromiley. Grand Rapids: Eerdmans, 1986.

Fackre, Gabriel. *The Religious Right and Christian Faith.* Grand Rapids: Eerdmans, 1982.

Falwell, Jerry. *Listen America!* Garden City, NY: Doubleday, 1980.

Foster, R. J. *Money, Sex and Power* (San Francisco: Harper & Row, 1985).

Frank, Douglas W. *Less Than Conquerors: How Evangelicals Entered the Twentieth Century.* Grand Rapids: Eerdmans, 1986.

Gallup, George, and D. Poling. *The Search for America's Faith.* Nashville: Abingdon, 1980.

Gaustad, Edwin S. "Did the Fundamentalists Win?" in M. Douglas and S. Tipton, *Religion and America.* Boston: Beacon Press, 1983.

Geisler, Norman, and Paul Feinberg. *Introduction to Philosophy.* Grand Rapids: Baker, 1980.

Griffith, Carol F., ed. *Christianity and Politics.* Washington, DC: Ethics & Public Policy Center, 1981.

Hadden, Jeffrey K., and A. Shupe. *Televangelism Power and Politics.* New York: Henry Holt, 1988. "No Time to Retreat," *Religious Broadcasting* (February 1988), pp. 66–68.

Hadden, Jeffrey K., and C. Swann. *Prime Time Preachers: The Rising Power of Televangelism.* Reading, MA: Addison-Wesley, 1981.

Halsell, Grace. *Prophecy and Politics: Militant Evangelists on the Road to Nuclear War.* Westport, CN: Lawrence Hill, 1986.

Hatch, Nathan, and Mark Noll, eds. *The Bible in America.* New York: Oxford University Press, 1982.

Source Notes

Henry, Carl F. H. *Christian Countermoves in a Decadent Culture*. Portland: Multnomah Press, 1986; *The Christian Mindset in a Secular Society*. Portland: Multnomah Press, 1984; "Lost Momentum: Carl F. H. Henry Looks at the Future of the Religious Right," *Christianity Today* (September 4, 1987), pp. 30–32; *The Uneasy Conscience of Modern Fundamentalism*. Grand Rapids: Eerdmans, 1947.

Hill, S. S., and D. E. Owen, *The New Religious Political Right*. Nashville: Abingdon, 1982.

Hindson, Ed. "The Mainline Is Becoming the Sideline," *Religious Broadcasting* (February 1988), pp. 22, 23; "Religion and Politics: Do They Mix?" *Religious Broadcasting* (January 1988), pp. 34, 35; "Thunder in the Pulpit: The Socio-Political Involvement of the New Right," *Foundations* (April–June 1982), pp. 144–152; *The Puritans' Use of Scripture in the Development of an Apocalyptical Hermeneutic*. Pretoria: University of South Africa, 1984; *Introduction to Puritan Theology*. Grand Rapids: Baker, 1976.

Horn, Carl, ed. *Whose Values? The Battle for Morality in Pluralistic America*. Ann Arbor, MI: Servant Books, 1985.

Hunt, Dave, and T. A. McMahon. *The Seduction of Christianity*. Eugene, OR: Harvest House, 1985.

Hunter, James D. *Evangelicalism: The Coming Generation*. Chicago: University of Chicago Press, 1987; *American Evangelicalism: Conservative Religion and the Quandary of Modernity*. New Brunswick, NJ: Rutgers University Press, 1983.

Hunter, Joel C. *Prayer, Politics and Power*. Wheaton, IL: Tyndale House, 1988.

Johnson, Paul. *Modern Times*. San Francisco: Harper & Row, 1983.

Johnston, Jon. *Will Evangelism Survive Its Own Popularity?* Grand Rapids: Zondervan, 1981.

Jorstad, Erling. *The Politics of Moralism: The New Christian Right in American Life*. Minneapolis: Augsburg, 1981.

Kelley, Dean. *Why Conservative Churches Are Growing*. New York: Harper & Row, 1972.

Kennedy, D. James. *Reconstruction: Biblical Guidelines for a Nation in Peril*. Ft. Lauderdale: Coral Ridge Ministries, 1986.

Kirk, Russell. "Promises and Perils of 'Christian Politics,' " *The Intercollegiate Review*, 18.1 (Fall 1982), pp. 13–24.

Kuitert, H. M. *Everything Is Politics but Politics Is Not Everything*. Grand Rapids: Eerdmans, 1986.

LaHaye, Tim. *The Race for the 21st Century*. Nashville: Thomas Nelson, 1986; *Faith of Our Founding Fathers*. Nashville: Wolgemuth & Hyatt, 1987; *The Battle for the Family*. Old Tappan, NJ: Revell, 1982; *The Battle for the Mind*. Old Tappan, NJ: Revell, 1980.

Langley, McKendree. "Robertson's Run: Going For It?" *Eternity* (September 1987), pp. 11–13; *The Practice of Political Spirituality*. Toronto: Paideia, 1984.

Liedman, K., and R. Wuthnow, eds. *The New Christian Right*. New York: Aldine, 1983.

Linder, R. D., and R. V. Pierard. *Twilight of the Saints: Biblical Christianity & Civil Religion in America*. Downers Grove, IL: Inter Varsity Press, 1978.

Lindsell, Harold. *The New Paganism: Understanding American Culture and the Role of the Church*. San Francisco: Harper & Row, 1987.

Lovelace, Richard. "Contemplating an Awakening," *Christian Century* (March 18, 1981), pp. 296–300.

Maguire, D. C. *The New Subversives: Anti-Americanism of the Religious Right*. New York: Continuum, 1982.

Marsden, George. *Fundamentalism and American Culture*. New York: Oxford University Press, 1980.

Marsden, George, ed. *Evangelicalism and Modern America*. Grand Rapids: Eerdmans, 1984.

Marshall, Paul. *Thine Is the Kingdom*. Grand Rapids: Eerdmans, 1984.

Marshall, Peter, and David Manuel. *The Light and the Glory*. Old Tappan, NJ: Revell, 1977; *From Sea to Shining Sea*. Old Tappan, NJ: Revell, 1986.

Martin, W. "The Birth of a Media Myth," *The Atlantic* (June 1981), pp. 7–16.

Marty, Martin. "Fundamentalism Reborn," *Saturday Review* (May 1980), pp. 35–40; "Insider's Look at Fundamentalism," *Christian Century* (November 18, 1981), pp. 1195–97; "Fundamentalism as a Social Phenomenon," *Review and Expositor* (Winter 1982), pp. 19–29.

McQuaid, Elwood. "What's Left for the Religious Right?" *Moody Monthly* (February 1988), pp. 12–17.

Stephen Monsma, *Pursuing Justice in a Sinful World*. Grand Rapids: Eerdmans, 1984.

Mouw, R. J. *Political Evangelicalism*. Grand Rapids: Eerdmans, 1973; *When Kings Come Marching In*. Grand Rapids: Eerdmans, 1983.

Nelson, Frank C. *Public Schools: An Evangelical Alternative*. Old Tappan, NJ: Revell, 1987.

Neuhaus, Richard J. *The Naked Public Square*. Grand Rapids: Eerdmans, 1984; "Who Now Will Shape the Meaning of America?" *Christianity Today* (March 19, 1982), pp. 16–20.

Neuhaus, Richard J., ed. *Unsecular America*. Grand Rapids: Eerdmans, 1986; *Virtue: Public and Private*. Grand Rapids: Eerdmans, 1986; *Confession, Conflict and Community*. Grand Rapids: Eerdmans, 1986; *Bible, Politics and Democracy*. Grand Rapids: Eerdmans, 1988.

Neuhaus, Richard J., and Michael Cromartie, *Piety and Politics: Evangelicals and Fundamentalists Confront the World*. Washington, DC: Ethics & Public Policy Center, 1987.

North, Gary. *Inherit the Earth*. Ft. Worth: Dominion Press, 1986.

Ostling, Richard N. "Jerry Falwell's Crusade," *Time* (September 2, 1985).

Paulk, Earl, *Ultimate Kingdom*. Atlanta: K-Dimension, 1984; *Held in the Heavens Until* . . . Atlanta: K-Dimension, 1985.

Ramm, Bernard. *After Fundamentalism: The Future of Evangelical Theology*. San Francisco: Harper & Row, 1983.

Reichley, A. J. *Religion in American Public Life*. Washington, DC: Brookings Institute, 1985.

Ribuffo, Leonard. *The Old Christian Right*. Philadelphia: Temple University Press, 1983.

Rothenberg, S., and F. Newport. *The Evangelical Voter*. Washington, DC: Free Congress Foundation, 1984.

Runner, H. Evan. *Scriptural Religion and Political Task*. Toronto: Wedge, 1974.

Rushdoony, R. J. *By What Standard?* Philadelphia: Presbyterian & Reformed, 1965; *Institutes of Biblical Law*. Fairfax, VA: Thoburn Press, 1965); *Thy Kingdom Come*. Fairfax, VA: Chalcedon, 1975.

Schaeffer, Francis A. *A Christian Manifesto*. Westchester, IL: Crossway Books, 1981; *The Great Evangelical Disaster*. Westchester, IL: Crossway Books, 1984; *How Should We Then Live?* Old Tappan, NJ: Revell, 1976.

Schaeffer, Francis A., and C. E. Koop. *Whatever Happened to the Human Race?* Old Tappan, NJ: Revell, 1979.

Shriver, Peggy. *The Bible Vote: Religion and the New Right*. New York: Pilgrim Press, 1981.

Sproul, R. C. *Lifeviews: Understanding the Ideas That Shape Society Today*. Old Tappan, NJ: Revell, 1986.

Stott, John. *Involvement: Being a Responsible Christian in a Non-Christian Society*, 2 vols. Old Tappan, NJ: Revell, 1984.

Sweet, Leonard. *The Evangelical Tradition in America*. Macon: Mercer University Press, 1984.

Thomas, Cal. *The Death of Ethics in America*. Waco, TX: Word Books, 1988; *Occupied Territory*. Nashville: Wolgemuth & Hyatt, 1987; *Liberals for Lunch*. Westchester, IL: Crossway Books, 1985; *Book Burning*. Westchester, IL: Crossway Books, 1983.

Viguerie, Richard. *The New Right: We're Ready to Lead*. Falls Church, VA: Viguerie Co., 1980.

Webber, Robert E. *The Church in the World*. Grand Rapids: Zondervan, 1986; *The Moral Majority: Right or Wrong?* Westchester, IL: Cornerstone Books, 1981.

Weber, Timothy P. *Living in the Shadow of the Second Coming: American Premillennialism 1875–1925*. New York: Oxford University Press, 1979.

Weyrich, Paul. "The Reagan Revolution That Wasn't," *Policy Review*, 41 (Summer 1987), pp. 50–53.

Whitehead, John W. *The Second American Revolution*. Elgin, IL: Cook Publishing, 1982.

Willimon, W. H. "The Chains of Religious Freedom," *Christianity Today* 31.13 (September 18, 1987), pp. 28–30.

Willoughby, William. *Does America Need the Moral Majority?* Plainfield, NJ: Logos Books, 1981.

Woodbridge, John D., et al. *The Gospel in America: Themes in the Story of America's Evangelicals*. Grand Rapids: Zondervan, 1979.

Woods, James, ed. *Religion and Politics*. Waco: Baylor University Press, 1983.

Zinsmeister, Karl. "The Revolt Against Alienation: A New Popular and Traditional Current Sweeps American Culture," *Policy Review*, 41 (Summer 1987), pp. 60–68.

Zwier, Robert. *Born Again Politics: The New Christian Right in America*. Downers Grove, IL: Inter Varsity Press, 1982.

INDEX

Ed Dobson is the senior pastor of Calvary Church in Grand Rapids, Michigan, and a noted conference speaker. He was formerly the Vice President of Liberty University in Lynchburg, Virginia, and editor of the *Fundamentalist Journal*. He holds the Ed.D. in Higher Education from the University of Virginia. **Ed Hindson** is the executive director of the Center for Biblical Counseling and Education in St. Louis, Missouri, and senior editor of *Religious Broadcasting*. He has lectured at numerous schools, including Oxford and Harvard and was formerly professor of religion at Liberty University. He holds the D.Min. from Westminster Theological Seminary and the D. Litt. et Phil. from the University of South Africa.